FACTSINATING

BIG book of fantastic facts you need to know!

Texas Harmon

Disclaimer

This book is intended for informational and educational purposes only. The facts, figures, and information presented herein have been compiled and presented with the utmost care and in good faith from various sources that are believed to be reliable and accurate at the time of writing.

However, the authors and publishers do not guarantee the accuracy, completeness, timeliness, or fitness for a particular purpose of the content herein. The information within this book is provided "as is," without warranty of any kind, either express or implied, including, but not limited to, implied warranties of merchantability or fitness for a particular purpose.

Readers should be aware that the field of knowledge is always expanding and evolving. Therefore, some information might become outdated or be reinterpreted in light of new evidence or perspectives after the publication of this book.

The authors and publishers expressly disclaim any responsibility for any liability, loss, or risk, personal or otherwise, which is incurred as a consequence, directly or indirectly, of the use and application of any of the contents of this book.

This book may also contain references to other publications, websites, or sources of information. Such references are not an endorsement of the third-party sources or their content.

Readers are encouraged to consult additional sources and exercise critical thinking when interpreting the facts and information in this book. The use of this book is at the reader's own risk.

CONTENTS

Astronomy & Space Exploration

Age of the Universe: The universe is approximately 13.8 billion years old, a timescale determined by measuring the expansion rate of the universe and the temperature of the cosmic microwave background radiation.

Vastness of Space: Space is unimaginably vast. The observable universe alone is about 93 billion light-years in diameter, filled with billions of galaxies, each containing billions of stars.

Human Footprints on the Moon: Humans first set foot on the Moon in 1969 during NASA's Apollo 11 mission. Since then, only 12 astronauts, all American, have walked on the lunar surface.

Mars Rovers: Various rovers have been sent to Mars to study its surface and atmosphere, searching for signs of past life and preparing for future human exploration.

Black Holes: Black holes are regions in space where gravity is so strong that nothing, not even light, can escape from them. They are key to understanding many aspects of astrophysics, including the lifecycle of stars.

The Sun's Power: The Sun, a medium-sized star, is the source of energy that sustains life on Earth. It's about 4.6 billion years old and has enough fuel to last about another 5 billion years.

Exoplanets and Alien Worlds: Thousands of planets have been discovered orbiting stars outside our solar system. These exoplanets are incredibly diverse and could potentially hold life.

The Hubble Space Telescope: Launched in 1990, the Hubble Space Telescope has provided some of the most detailed images of distant galaxies, nebulae, and other astronomical phenomena, revolutionizing our understanding of the universe.

International Space Station (ISS): The ISS is a symbol of international cooperation in space, a research laboratory orbiting Earth where astronauts conduct experiments in various scientific fields.

Voyager Probes: The Voyager probes, launched in the 1970s, have traveled further into space than any other human-made objects. They carry with them the Golden Records, which contain sounds and images representing life and culture on Earth.

Ancient Civilizations

Cradles of Civilization: The earliest civilizations arose in fertile river valleys, including Mesopotamia in the Tigris-Euphrates valley, Ancient Egypt in the Nile valley, the Indus Valley civilization in modern-day Pakistan and India, and ancient China along the Yellow River.

Mesopotamia's Innovations: Often called the cradle of

civilization, Mesopotamia, located in present-day Iraq, saw the emergence of some of the first cities, writing systems (cuneiform), and the wheel.

Egypt's Architectural Marvels: Ancient Egypt is renowned for its monumental architecture, including the pyramids and the Great Sphinx of Giza. These structures were mainly built as tombs for the country's pharaohs and are a testament to their engineering skills.

Indus Valley's Urban Planning: The Indus Valley Civilization, dating back to 2600 BCE, was notable for its advanced urban planning, including well-organized cities with sophisticated sewage systems.

Ancient China's Contributions: Ancient China made significant contributions to the world, including the invention of paper, gunpowder, the compass, and printing technology.

Greece - The Birthplace of Western Civilization: Ancient Greece is often considered the birthplace of Western civilization. It contributed immensely to the fields of philosophy, history, drama, and science.

Roman Engineering and Law: The Romans were known for their remarkable engineering feats, including roads, aqueducts, and the Colosseum. They also laid down legal codes that influence legal systems to this day.

Mayan Scientific Achievements: The ancient Maya, known for their sophisticated calendar and writing system, were also skilled astronomers, mathematicians, and architects.

Trade and Cultural Exchange: Ancient civilizations were not isolated. There was significant trade and cultural exchange along routes like the Silk Road, which connected China to the Mediterranean.

Mysterious Decline: Many ancient civilizations declined under mysterious circumstances, with theories ranging from environmental changes to invasions and societal collapse.

Sophisticated Harappan Cities: The Harappan civilization, part of the Indus Valley civilization, is known for its highly sophisticated and technologically advanced urban culture. Cities like Harappa and Mohenjo-Daro had well-planned streets, brick houses, and an elaborate drainage system.

Egyptian Hieroglyphs: Ancient Egyptians used a writing system of pictorial symbols called hieroglyphs. Deciphering these was a mystery until the discovery of the Rosetta Stone, which helped unlock the secrets of this ancient script.

Babylonian Mathematics: The Babylonians, another Mesopotamian civilization, are known for their contributions to mathematics, especially their development of an early form of algebra and a sophisticated number system based on 60, which is the basis for our 60-second minute and 60-minute hour.

Greek Philosophy and Democracy: Ancient Greece was the birthplace of Western philosophy, with philosophers like Socrates, Plato, and Aristotle laying the foundations of Western thought. Athens, a city-state in Greece, is also considered the birthplace of democracy.

Roman Roads and Infrastructure: The Romans built an

extensive network of roads that connected their vast empire. These roads were so well-constructed that some are still in use today. They also built impressive aqueducts to supply their cities with fresh water.

Mayan Calendar: The Mayan calendar was highly complex and accurate. It included various cycles of time to track religious and astronomical events. The Long Count calendar, which tracked longer periods, famously reset in 2012, leading to many modern misconceptions about Mayan prophecies.

Chinese Inventions: Besides paper, printing, and gunpowder, ancient China also invented silk, porcelain, and the crossbow. The Han Dynasty (206 BCE – 220 CE) saw significant advances in science, technology, and mathematics.

Aztec Empire: The Aztecs, based in what is now Mexico, built a powerful empire known for its impressive pyramids, human sacrifices, and advanced agricultural practices, including the chinampa system or "floating gardens."

Stonehenge Mystery: In ancient Britain, Stonehenge was constructed in several stages, with the earliest dating back to about 3000 BCE. Its purpose remains a subject of debate, ranging from a religious temple to an astronomical observatory.

Ancient Libraries: The Library of Alexandria in Egypt and the Library of Ashurbanipal in Mesopotamia were among the largest and most significant libraries of the ancient world, housing thousands of scrolls and texts.

World Oceans and Marine Life

Five Major Oceans: Earth's surface is covered by five major oceans – the Pacific, Atlantic, Indian, Southern, and Arctic. The Pacific Ocean is the largest and deepest, containing more than half of the world's free water.

Great Barrier Reef: Located in the Coral Sea, off the coast of Australia, the Great Barrier Reef is the world's largest coral reef system. It's home to thousands of species of marine life and is visible from space.

Deepest Point in the Oceans: The Mariana Trench, located in the western Pacific Ocean, is the deepest part of the world's oceans, reaching a depth of about 36,070 feet (10,994 meters). It's deeper than the height of Mount Everest.

Marine Biodiversity: Oceans are incredibly biodiverse, hosting millions of species, many of which are yet to be discovered. This includes tiny plankton, fish, turtles, sharks, whales, and deep-sea creatures.

Ocean Currents: The oceans are crisscrossed by a complex network of currents that move water around the globe. These currents play a crucial role in regulating the Earth's climate by transferring heat from the equator to the poles.

Mysterious Deep Sea: The deep sea, below 200 meters, remains largely unexplored. It's a realm of extreme conditions, pitch darkness, and home to some of the most unusual life forms on Earth, many adapted to high pressure and low temperatures.

Importance of Plankton: Plankton, both phytoplankton (plants) and zooplankton (animals), are the foundation of the oceanic food chain. Phytoplankton also produce over half of the world's oxygen through photosynthesis.

Marine Migration: Many marine species undertake long migrations for feeding and breeding. The Arctic tern, for instance, migrates over 25,000 miles annually, the longest known migration of any animal.

Threats to Marine Life: Oceans face numerous threats, including pollution, overfishing, invasive species, and climate change, which result in habitat destruction and loss of biodiversity.

Ocean Exploration: Despite being a crucial part of our planet, more than 80% of the world's oceans remain unexplored and unmapped, offering a vast frontier for discovery and research.

Mangrove Forests: Mangroves are unique ecosystems found at the interface between land and sea in tropical regions. They provide critical habitat for a diverse array of wildlife and help protect coastlines from erosion and storm surges.

Marine Mammals: The oceans are home to a wide variety of marine mammals, including dolphins, whales, seals, and manatees. Many of these mammals have complex brains and exhibit sophisticated behaviors like social bonding, communication, and tool use.

Hydrothermal Vents: These are fissures on the seafloor that emit hot, mineral-rich water. They create unique ecosystems deep in the ocean, hosting organisms that rely on chemosynthesis, a process of converting chemical energy into food, instead of photosynthesis.

Phenomenon of Bioluminescence: Many marine organisms, like certain fish, jellyfish, and plankton, exhibit bioluminescence – the ability to produce light through chemical reactions. This adaptation is used for various purposes, including camouflage, attracting prey, and communication.

Coral Bleaching: This occurs when corals, stressed by changes in conditions such as temperature, light, or nutrients, expel the symbiotic algae living in their tissues, causing them to turn completely white. This can lead to coral death and the deterioration of coral reef ecosystems.

The Ocean's Blue Color: The ocean appears blue because water absorbs colors in the red part of the light spectrum and reflects the blue part. This is why the ocean can appear a deep blue in areas with very pure water.

Saltwater and Freshwater Mixing: Estuaries are bodies of water where freshwater from rivers meets and mixes with saltwater from the ocean. These areas are biologically productive and provide important habitats for many species.

Tsunamis: These are large, powerful waves caused by disturbances such as underwater earthquakes, volcanic eruptions, or landslides. Tsunamis can travel across entire ocean basins and cause extensive damage when they hit coastlines.

The Importance of Seagrasses: Seagrass meadows are important oceanic ecosystems. They provide habitats, nursery grounds for many marine species, help stabilize sediment, and play a role in carbon sequestration.

Icebergs and Glaciers: Parts of the polar regions, icebergs and glaciers are significant features of the marine ecosystem. They are freshwater sources and affect ocean currents, and their melting patterns are crucial indicators of climate change.

Inventions & Discoveries

The Wheel: One of the earliest and most significant inventions, the wheel was invented more than 5,000 years ago. It not only revolutionized transportation but also machines and technology as a whole.

Penicillin: Discovered by Alexander Fleming in 1928, penicillin was the world's first true antibiotic. It has saved countless lives by treating bacterial infections and marked the beginning of a new era in medicine.

The Internet: Initially a project called ARPANET developed in the late 1960s for the U.S. Department of Defense, the internet has evolved into a global system of interconnected networks that has transformed communication, information sharing, and commerce.

Electricity: The discovery and harnessing of electricity have been fundamental to the modern world. Figures like Thomas Edison, Nikola Tesla, and Michael Faraday were pivotal in bringing electricity into homes and industries.

DNA Structure: The discovery of the DNA double helix by James Watson and Francis Crick in 1953 revolutionized biology and medicine. Understanding DNA's structure opened doors to genetic research, biotechnology, and forensic science.

The Printing Press: Invented by Johannes Gutenberg in the mid-15th century, the printing press allowed for the mass production of books and was instrumental in spreading knowledge, contributing to the Renaissance and the Scientific Revolution.

The Airplane: The Wright brothers' first successful flight in 1903 brought about a new era in transportation and changed the course of world history, making global travel and international connections possible.

Vaccination: The concept of vaccination was revolutionized by Edward Jenner in 1796 with the smallpox vaccine. It set the stage for modern immunology and has led to the eradication and control of numerous deadly diseases.

Radioactivity: Discovered by Henri Becquerel and further researched by Marie and Pierre Curie, radioactivity's discovery in the late 19th century led to significant developments in energy, medicine, and science.

The Telescope: Invented in the early 17th century, the telescope opened up the universe for exploration. It led to crucial discoveries in astronomy, including the observation of the moons of Jupiter by Galileo, which challenged established views of the cosmos.

Slinky: This simple toy was actually invented by accident by an engineer named Richard James in 1943. He was working to develop springs that could support and stabilize sensitive equipment on ships during World War II when he noticed the entertaining way one of the springs moved.

Microwave Oven: The microwave oven was also a product of accidental discovery. In 1945, engineer Percy Spencer noticed a candy bar melting in his pocket while working on radar technology, leading to the invention of the microwave oven.

Velcro: Inspired by the way burrs stuck to his dog's fur, Swiss engineer George de Mestral invented Velcro in the 1940s. It took nearly a decade to perfect the design, but it became a popular fastener worldwide.

Post-it Notes: In 1968, a scientist at 3M, Dr. Spencer Silver, was attempting to develop a super-strong adhesive. Instead, he accidentally created a low-tack, reusable pressure-sensitive adhesive, leading to the creation of Post-it Notes.

Saccharin: This artificial sweetener was discovered accidentally in 1879 by Constantin Fahlberg, a chemist who noticed a sweet taste on his hand after a day's work in the lab and traced it back to an experiment.

The Pacemaker: The first wearable pacemaker was invented somewhat accidentally in 1957. While working on a heart rhythm recording device, Wilson Greatbatch grabbed the wrong resistor and inserted it into the circuit, which then started to emit a rhythm that mimicked the human heart.

Safety Glass: Safety glass, now commonly used in car windshields, was discovered accidentally by French chemist Édouard Bénédictus in 1903. He dropped a glass flask coated with cellulose nitrate, which cracked but did not shatter, inspiring the idea.

X-Rays: In 1895, German physicist Wilhelm Conrad Röntgen was experimenting with cathode rays when he discovered a new type of ray that could pass through most substances, including the human body, leading to the invention of the X-ray.

Dynamite: Alfred Nobel, who later established the Nobel Prizes, invented dynamite in 1867. He was trying to make nitroglycerin safer to handle after a deadly explosion in his factory.

LSD: Lysergic acid diethylamide, or LSD, was synthesized by Swiss chemist Albert Hofmann in 1938 while researching medicinal uses for ergot, a fungus. He accidentally discovered its psychedelic effects five years later.

World Geography

Mariana Trench: The Mariana Trench is the deepest part of the world's oceans, located in the western Pacific Ocean. It reaches a depth of about 36,070 feet (10,994 meters), deeper than Mount Everest is tall.

Amazon River: Often debated as the world's longest river (alongside the Nile), the Amazon River in South America is by far the largest by water flow, discharging more water than the next seven largest rivers combined.

Sahara Desert Expansion: The Sahara, the world's largest hot desert, is expanding. It has grown by about 10% in the past century, partly due to climate change and human activities affecting land use.

Himalayas Growth: The Himalayas, home to Mount Everest, the world's highest peak, are still growing taller. The collision of the Indian and Eurasian tectonic plates causes the range to rise about 5 mm per year.

Dead Sea's Uniqueness: The Dead Sea, bordering Israel, the West Bank, and Jordan, is the lowest point on dry land and one of the saltiest bodies of water in the world. This salinity makes it easy for people to float, and its mud is renowned for its health benefits.

Lake Baikal: Located in Siberia, Russia, Lake Baikal is the world's deepest and oldest freshwater lake. It contains about 20% of the world's unfrozen freshwater reserve and is known for its unique biodiversity.

Great Barrier Reef Size: The Great Barrier Reef off the coast of Australia is the world's largest coral reef system and the only living structure on Earth visible from space. It spans over 2,300 kilometers and includes thousands of reefs and hundreds of islands.

Danakil Depression: The Danakil Depression in Ethiopia is one of the hottest and most alien places on Earth. This area is known for its vibrant colors, extreme heat, and active volcanoes, making it look more like a Martian landscape.

Antarctica's Dry Valleys: The McMurdo Dry Valleys in Antarctica are the driest places on Earth. These valleys haven't seen rain for nearly 2 million years, making them a unique scientific and geographical phenomenon.

Greenland's Ice Sheet: Greenland's ice sheet is the largest mass of ice in the northern hemisphere, covering 1.7 million square kilometers. If it were to melt entirely, global sea levels would rise by about 7 meters.

Angel Falls: Located in Venezuela, Angel Falls is the world's highest uninterrupted waterfall, with a height of 979 meters (3,212 feet) and a plunge of 807 meters (2,648 feet). The falls are named after Jimmy Angel, a U.S. aviator who was the first to fly over them.

The Ring of Fire: Encircling the Pacific Ocean, the Ring of Fire is a horseshoe-shaped zone with a high concentration of active volcanoes and frequent earthquakes. It's home to about 75% of the world's active and dormant volcanoes.

Mount Thor: Found in Canada's Auyuittuq National Park, Mount Thor boasts the world's greatest vertical drop of 1,250 meters (4,101 feet). It's a dream destination for extreme climbers, known for its challenging ascent and sheer drop.

Socotra Island: Located off the coast of Yemen, Socotra Island is one of the most isolated landforms on Earth of continental origin. It's home to unique flora and fauna, with about one-third of its plant life being found nowhere else on the planet.

Salar de Uyuni: In Bolivia, Salar de Uyuni is the world's largest salt flat, created by prehistoric lakes that evaporated long ago. After a rain, the salt flat becomes the world's largest natural mirror, reflecting the sky.

Lake Hillier: This remarkable lake on Middle Island, off the coast of Western Australia, is famous for its pink color. The color is due to the presence of algae and bacteria that produce carotenoids, which give the lake its unique hue.

The Amazon Rainforest: The Amazon Rainforest, spanning across nine countries in South America, is the largest tropical rainforest in the world. It's home to an estimated 390 billion individual trees and 16,000 species.

Pamukkale Thermal Pools: In southwestern Turkey, Pamukkale, meaning "cotton castle" in Turkish, is famous for its white terraces formed by calcite-rich thermal waters. The site has been used as a spa since the second century BCE.

The Atacama Desert: Stretching along the Pacific coast of Chile, the Atacama Desert is the driest non-polar desert in the world. Some weather stations in the Atacama have never recorded rain.

The Alps' Age: The Alps, Europe's greatest mountain range, are relatively young in geological terms. They formed about 65 million years ago as the African and Eurasian tectonic plates collided.

Famous Historical Figures

Leonardo da Vinci: Known as a true Renaissance man, da Vinci was ambidextrous. He could write with one hand and draw with the other simultaneously. His notebooks are filled with mirror writing, a script that is a reverse of the normal writing.

Cleopatra: The last active ruler of the Ptolemaic Kingdom of

Egypt, Cleopatra was not actually Egyptian but Greek. She was a member of the Ptolemaic dynasty, a family of Greek origin that ruled Egypt after Alexander the Great's death.

Albert Einstein: Renowned physicist Albert Einstein was offered the presidency of Israel in 1952. He declined the offer, stating that he lacked the necessary experience in dealing with human affairs.

Genghis Khan: One of history's greatest conquerors, Genghis Khan, left such a genetic legacy that about 1 in 200 men today are genetic descendants of him, according to some studies. His conquests reshaped the world in the 13th century.

Marie Curie: A pioneer in radioactivity, Marie Curie was the first woman to win a Nobel Prize and the only person to win a Nobel in two different sciences (Physics and Chemistry). She also developed mobile radiography units to provide X-ray services to field hospitals during World War I.

Mozart: Wolfgang Amadeus Mozart was a musical prodigy who began composing at the age of five. His compositions were often characterized by a lightness and grace, which contrasted with the more complex and serious compositions of his time.

Joan of Arc: A peasant girl living in medieval France, Joan of Arc believed that God had chosen her to lead France to victory in its long-running war with England. She was eventually captured, tried, and executed, but her legend lived on, leading to her canonization as a saint.

Isaac Newton: Best known for his laws of motion and universal gravitation, Isaac Newton also made significant contributions to optics and shares credit with Gottfried Wilhelm Leibniz for developing calculus.

Queen Elizabeth I: Known as the Virgin Queen, Elizabeth I was the last of the five monarchs of the House of Tudor. Her reign of 44 years is known as the Elizabethan era and was marked by the flourishing of English drama, led by playwrights such as William Shakespeare.

Nikola Tesla: An inventor, electrical engineer, and futurist, Tesla developed the basis for alternating current (AC) power systems. He envisioned a world of free, wireless electricity and worked on experiments to transmit electrical energy without wires.

Thomas Edison: Known for inventing the light bulb, Edison held over 1,000 patents. He also created the world's first industrial research laboratory and had a rivalry with Nikola Tesla over electrical systems.

Rosa Parks: A pivotal figure in the American Civil Rights Movement, Rosa Parks' refusal to give up her seat on a segregated bus was not her first act of defiance. She had a history of quietly but firmly resisting racial segregation.

Alexander the Great: One of the world's most successful military commanders, Alexander the Great was never defeated in battle. By the age of 30, he had created one of the largest empires of the ancient world, stretching from Greece to northwestern India.

Frida Kahlo: A renowned Mexican artist known for her

captivating self-portraits, Frida Kahlo began painting after a severe accident. Her works are celebrated for their vivid colors and honest depictions of her life and pain.

Winston Churchill: A British statesman and Prime Minister during World War II, Churchill was also a Nobel Prize-winning author and an accomplished painter. He is remembered for his leadership, oratory skills, and determination during the war.

Amelia Earhart: The first female aviator to fly solo across the Atlantic Ocean, Amelia Earhart was a pioneer in aviation and a symbol of the aspirations of women in the early 20th century. Her disappearance during a circumnavigational flight attempt remains a mystery.

Shakespeare: William Shakespeare, often regarded as the greatest writer in the English language, contributed over 1,700 words to the English language. His plays and sonnets have transcended time and culture, with themes that remain relevant today.

Galileo Galilei: An Italian astronomer, physicist, and engineer, Galileo is often called the "father of observational astronomy," the "father of modern physics," and the "father of the scientific method." His support for heliocentrism was controversial during his time, leading to an inquisition and house arrest.

Socrates: A classical Greek philosopher, Socrates is known as one of the founders of Western philosophy. Interestingly, he never wrote down his teachings; our knowledge of his ideas and methods comes from his students, like Plato.

Animal Kingdom

Migratory Marvels: The Arctic tern has the longest migration of any animal. It travels from the Arctic to the Antarctic and back again each year, a round trip of about 25,000 miles.

Deep Sea Mysteries: The colossal squid, living in the deep ocean, is one of the largest known invertebrates. It can reach lengths of up to 46 feet and has the largest eyes in the animal kingdom.

Camouflage Experts: The chameleon is famous for its ability to change color for camouflage, communication, and temperature regulation. This color change is achieved through special cells in their skin called chromatophores.

Insect Architects: Termites are remarkable architects. Some species build mounds up to 30 feet tall, featuring a complex system of tunnels and chambers for ventilation and temperature control.

Birds of Prey: The peregrine falcon is the fastest bird, reaching speeds over 200 miles per hour during its hunting stoop (high-speed dive), making it the fastest member of the animal kingdom.

Marine Intelligence: Dolphins are known for their high intelligence, complex social structures, and ability to communicate using a variety of clicks and whistles. They also demonstrate self-awareness, problem-solving skills, and empathy.

Longevity in the Sea: The Greenland shark has one of the longest lifespans of any animal, living up to 400 years. They grow only about a centimeter a year, reaching maturity at around 150 years old.

Social Insects: Honeybees live in well-organized colonies that can contain up to 60,000 bees. They communicate through dances and pheromones and are vital pollinators for many plants.

Amphibian Diversity: The poison dart frog, found in Central and South American rainforests, has brightly colored skin that is toxic. These vibrant colors warn predators of their toxicity.

Gentle Giants: Elephants are the largest land animals, known for their complex social structures, long memories, and strong familial bonds. They communicate using low-frequency sounds that can travel several miles.

Bioluminescent Wonders: The firefly, a type of beetle, produces light through a chemical reaction in its abdomen. This bioluminescence is used for communication, especially during mating rituals.

Architectural Achievements: Beavers are known for their natural skill in building dams and lodges. Their constructions can alter the ecosystem, creating wetlands beneficial to many species.

Bird Intelligence: The African grey parrot is renowned for its intelligence and ability to mimic human speech. These parrots have shown cognitive abilities at the level of dolphins, apes, and even young human children in some studies.

Incredible Invertebrates: The octopus is highly intelligent, capable of problem-solving and complex navigation. They can also change color and texture to blend into their surroundings, and some species display remarkable escape artist skills.

Desert Survivalists: The camel, well-adapted to life in harsh desert conditions, can go for long periods without water. They store fat in their humps, not water, which can be converted to water and energy when resources are scarce.

Majestic Migrators: Monarch butterflies undertake an incredible migration of up to 3,000 miles from North America to central Mexico, a journey that spans multiple generations.

Deep Dive Champions: The sperm whale holds the record for the deepest and longest dive among mammals. They can dive over 2,000 meters deep and stay submerged for up to 90 minutes.

Social Networks of Elephants: Elephants have complex social structures and demonstrate behaviors like empathy, mourning, and self-awareness. They use a variety of sounds and seismic vibrations to communicate over long distances.

Polar Survival: Polar bears, the largest land carnivores, are expertly adapted to the Arctic environment. Their fur provides insulation, and their large paws help distribute weight on thin ice.

Speedy Predators: The cheetah is the fastest land animal, capable of speeds up to 75 mph in short bursts covering distances up to 1,500 feet, with exceptional acceleration.

Plant Life & Botany

Giant Sequoias and Redwoods: The giant sequoias and redwoods of California are some of the largest and oldest living organisms on Earth. Some of these trees are over 3,000 years old, reaching heights of more than 300 feet.

Carnivorous Plants: The Venus flytrap, native to subtropical wetlands in the U.S., is one of the few plants capable of rapid movement, snapping shut to capture insects and spiders for nutrients typically scarce in their environments.

Plant Communication: Plants can communicate with each other through underground networks of fungi known as mycorrhizae. This "wood wide web" allows them to share resources and even warn each other of potential threats.

Survivors of the Desert: The Welwitschia mirabilis, found in the Namib Desert, is one of the most resilient and longest-living plants. It can live for over 1,000 years and has only two leaves that grow continuously over its lifetime.

Oxygen Providers: Phytoplankton, tiny marine plants, contribute between 50% to 85% of the oxygen in Earth's atmosphere. They are as crucial as the land-based plants for maintaining the oxygen level.

Medicinal Plants: Many modern medicines are derived from plants. For example, aspirin originated from compounds found in the bark of willow trees.

Remarkable Adaptations: The lotus plant has superhydrophobic leaves, meaning they are extremely water-repellent. This adaptation helps them stay clean, as water droplets roll off, taking dirt with them.

The Oldest Seed to Germinate: A date palm seed from Masada, an ancient fortress in Israel, was successfully germinated after about 2,000 years, making it the oldest known seed to sprout.

Solar Power Efficiency: Plants are incredibly efficient at capturing the sun's energy. In photosynthesis, they use sunlight to convert water and carbon dioxide into oxygen and glucose, a process that fuels their growth and provides energy to the food chain.

Rafflesia Arnoldii: This plant, found in Southeast Asian rainforests, produces the largest individual flower in the world. It can grow over three feet across and emits a strong odor of decaying flesh, earning it the nickname "corpse flower."

The Intelligence of Plants: Research suggests that plants can exhibit intelligent behavior, despite lacking brains. They can sense their environment, respond to sound, and even exhibit memory-like responses.

Ancient Trees: The Methuselah tree, a bristlecone pine located in California's White Mountains, is one of the oldest living trees in the world. Its age is over 4,800 years, making it older than most human civilizations.

Bamboo's Rapid Growth: Some species of bamboo are the fastest-growing plants in the world. They can grow up to 35 inches per day, which is almost 1.5 inches an hour!

The Sensitive Plant: Mimosa pudica, commonly known as the sensitive plant, quickly closes its leaves when touched. This is thought to be a defense mechanism to scare away potential predators.

Aeroplankton: Just like phytoplankton in the oceans, there's aeroplankton in the air – tiny airborne algae and moss spores. They are an essential part of the atmosphere's ecosystem.

Photosynthesis Underwater: Seagrasses are the only flowering plants capable of living and performing photosynthesis entirely underwater. They play a critical role in coastal ecosystems and carbon sequestration.

Parasitic Plants: The Rafflesia and the corpse flower aren't the only oddities. Parasitic plants like the dodder lack chlorophyll and derive nutrients by attaching themselves to host plants.

Plants in Space: NASA has experimented with growing plants in space. These studies help understand how plants adapt in microgravity and contribute to long-term human space exploration by providing food and oxygen.

The "Living Fossil" Plant: The Ginkgo biloba tree, native to China, is often referred to as a living fossil. It's the only surviving member of an ancient order of plants, with fossils dating back 270 million years.

Floral Giants: The Titan arum, another "corpse flower," produces the world's largest unbranched inflorescence, with the flower structure reaching over 10 feet in height.

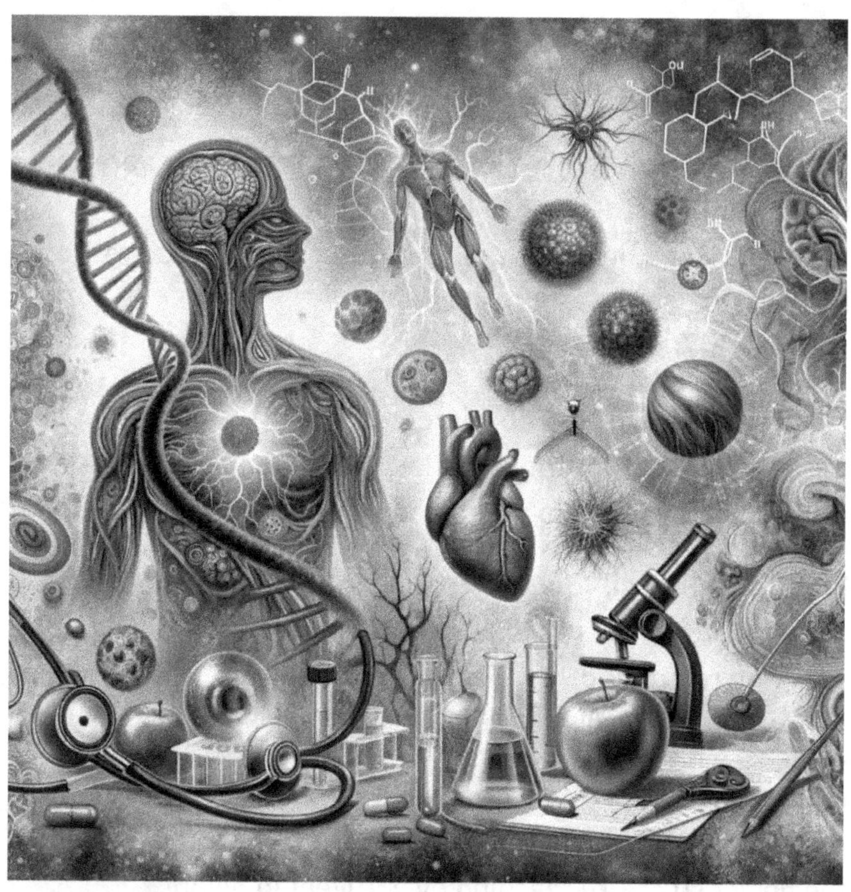

Human Body & Medicine

The Brain's Power: The human brain is one of the most complex structures in the known universe. It contains approximately 86 billion neurons, each with the potential to make thousands of synaptic connections.

Regenerative Skin: Our skin is the body's largest organ and has remarkable regenerative abilities. An average person may shed and regrow their outer skin layer every 27 days.

Heart's Lifelong Work: The heart is an extraordinary organ; it beats about 100,000 times a day and pumps nearly 1.5 gallons of blood every minute. Over an average lifetime, that's more than 2.5 billion beats!

Bone Strength: Human bones are incredibly strong. Ounce for ounce, some bones can bear more weight than steel.

Genetic Uniqueness: Except for identical twins, each person's DNA is unique. This genetic complexity makes each individual distinctive in appearance and health.

Immune System Complexity: The human immune system is an advanced defense mechanism. It can recognize millions of different enemies and can produce powerful chemicals and cells to protect us.

Microbiome Diversity: Our bodies are home to trillions of microbes, collectively known as the microbiome. These bacteria play crucial roles in digestion, immunity, and even mental health.

Fingerprint Uniqueness: Every person's fingerprint is unique, making it an essential tool for identification. Even identical twins have different fingerprints.

The Power of Vaccines: Vaccines have revolutionized medicine, leading to the eradication of diseases like smallpox and drastically reducing the incidence of many others, such as polio and measles.

The Eye's Complexity: The human eye can distinguish about

10 million different colors. It's so sensitive that, under the right conditions, it can see the light of a candle at a distance of 14 miles.

Blood Vessel Length: If laid end to end, an adult's blood vessels could circle Earth's equator four times, spanning a total of nearly 100,000 miles.

Sensory Richness of Taste: Humans can taste a wide range of flavors, and each taste bud contains 50 to 100 taste receptor cells, responding to different tastes like sweet, sour, salty, bitter, and umami.

Liver's Regenerative Ability: The liver has an extraordinary capacity to regenerate. As much as 75% of the liver can be removed, and it can still regrow to its full size.

Complexity of the Hand: The human hand is incredibly complex, comprising 27 bones, 29 joints, and at least 123 named ligaments. This complexity allows for a wide range of movements and functions.

The Persistence of Memory Cells: Some memory cells in the immune system can remember an encountered pathogen for decades, which is the basis for the long-lasting protection of vaccines.

Lungs' Surface Area: If the lungs' alveoli - tiny sacs where oxygen and carbon dioxide are exchanged - were spread out flat, they would cover an area roughly the size of a tennis court.

The Human Genome Project: Completed in 2003, this project mapped the entire human genome, comprising about 20,500 genes. This monumental achievement has revolutionized medicine and genetics.

Incredible Speed of Nerve Impulses: Nerve impulses travel to and from the brain at speeds up to 250 miles per hour, showcasing the body's rapid response system.

Ear's Fine Mechanics: The smallest bones in the human body are in the ear (the malleus, incus, and stapes) and are crucial for transmitting sound vibrations to the inner ear.

Advances in Prosthetics: Modern prosthetics have advanced tremendously, with some now capable of being controlled by the mind, responding to electrical impulses from muscles, or providing sensory feedback.

Physics & The Laws of Nature

Relativity of Time: According to Einstein's theory of relativity, time is relative and can vary depending on speed and gravity. This means that time passes differently in space than it does on Earth.

Quantum Entanglement: In quantum physics, particles can become entangled and instantaneously affect each other regardless of distance, a phenomenon Einstein famously referred to as "spooky action at a distance."

The Uncertainty Principle: Heisenberg's uncertainty principle states that we cannot simultaneously know the exact position and momentum of a particle. This principle is a fundamental concept of quantum mechanics.

The Speed of Light: The speed of light in a vacuum is a constant 299,792,458 meters per second. Nothing in the universe can travel faster than light.

Black Holes and Event Horizons: Black holes are regions in space where gravity is so strong that nothing, not even light, can escape from them. The event horizon is the point around a black hole beyond which no return is possible.

Wave-Particle Duality: Quantum theory proposes that every particle or quantum entity can be partly described in terms not only of particles but also of waves. This duality addresses the inadequacy of conventional concepts like "particle" and "wave" in fully describing the behavior of quantum-scale objects.

The Four Fundamental Forces: The universe is governed by four fundamental forces: gravity, electromagnetism, the strong nuclear force, and the weak nuclear force. These forces govern the interactions of all matter and energy.

The Big Bang Theory: The Big Bang Theory is the leading explanation about how the universe began. It suggests that the universe was once incredibly small and dense before rapidly expanding.

Energy Conservation: The law of conservation of energy states that energy cannot be created or destroyed, only transformed from one form to another. This principle is fundamental in all branches of physics.

The Mystery of Dark Matter and Dark Energy: Dark matter and dark energy are theoretical forms of matter and energy thought to make up 95% of the universe. They are invisible and undetectable by existing instruments, but their presence is inferred from gravitational effects on visible matter.

Superconductivity: Superconductors are materials that can conduct electricity without resistance when cooled to very low temperatures. This remarkable property has significant implications for energy transmission and magnetic levitation.

The Higgs Boson: Often referred to as the "God particle," the Higgs boson is a fundamental particle associated with the Higgs field, which gives other particles their mass. Its discovery in 2012 was a monumental event in particle physics.

Antimatter: For every particle, there exists an antiparticle with the same mass but opposite charge. When matter and antimatter meet, they annihilate each other, releasing energy. Understanding antimatter is key to exploring the asymmetry in the universe.

Neutron Stars: These incredibly dense remnants of supernova explosions are so compact that a sugar-cube-sized amount of neutron star material would weigh about a billion tons on Earth.

Fermi Paradox and the Search for Extraterrestrial Life: The

Fermi Paradox grapples with the contradiction between the high probability of extraterrestrial life and the lack of evidence for, or contact with, such civilizations.

The Double-Slit Experiment: This experiment demonstrates that light and matter can display characteristics of both classically defined waves and particles; the observation or measurement itself affects the outcome.

Schwarzschild Radius and Black Holes: The Schwarzschild radius is the size at which an object's escape velocity equals the speed of light, forming a black hole. This concept is crucial in the study of astrophysics and black holes.

Thermodynamics Laws: The laws of thermodynamics govern the principles of energy transfer and entropy. They are fundamental in understanding not just physics, but chemistry, biology, and even economics.

String Theory: String theory is a theoretical framework in which the point-like particles of particle physics are replaced by one-dimensional "strings." It's a leading candidate for a theory of everything, aiming to reconcile gravity and quantum mechanics.

Plasma, the Fourth State of Matter: Often overlooked, plasma is the most abundant form of matter in the universe. It consists of a hot, ionized gas found in stars, including the sun, and is used in technologies like fluorescent lights and plasma TVs.

Chemical Elements & Compounds

Oxygen's Vital Role: Oxygen, the third most abundant element in the universe by mass, is essential for respiration in most living organisms. It also makes up 21% of Earth's atmosphere.

Helium's Lightness: Helium is the second lightest and second most abundant element in the observable universe. It is so light that Earth's gravity is not strong enough to hold it, and it escapes into space.

Carbon's Versatility: Carbon is the basis for all known life on Earth, capable of forming almost ten million different compounds. It exists in several forms, including graphite, diamond, and amorphous carbon.

Hydrogen's Abundance: Hydrogen is the most abundant chemical substance in the universe, constituting roughly 75% of all normal matter. It is the primary fuel for stars, including the sun.

Gold's Rarity and Malleability: Gold is one of the least reactive chemical elements and is solid under standard conditions. It is so malleable that one gram can be beaten into a sheet of one square meter.

Water's Anomalies: Water is the only natural substance found in all three physical states – liquid, solid, and gas – at the temperatures that occur within Earth's atmosphere.

The Noble Gases: The noble gases, including helium, neon, and argon, are inert and rarely form compounds. They are used in various applications like lighting, welding, and space exploration due to their stability.

Sodium and Chlorine's Transformation: Alone, sodium and chlorine are dangerous elements, but combined, they form sodium chloride – table salt – essential for human life.

The Periodic Table's Organization: The periodic table

organizes 118 elements by their chemical properties. Dmitri Mendeleev created the first widely recognized periodic table in 1869.

Uranium's Power: Uranium, a dense metal, is used as fuel in nuclear power plants. Its discovery in 1789 by Martin Heinrich Klaproth led to the development of nuclear energy and weapons.

Iodine's Color Change: Iodine is a unique element that sublimates, changing directly from a solid to a gas without becoming liquid. When it sublimates, it produces a beautiful violet vapor.

Mercury's Liquid State: Mercury is the only metal that is liquid at standard room temperature and pressure. Its ability to remain liquid has made it useful in devices like thermometers and barometers.

The Rarity of Astatine: Astatine is the rarest naturally occurring element in the Earth's crust. It is estimated that the Earth's crust contains less than 1 ounce of astatine, making it extremely rare and radioactive.

Silicon's Role in Technology: Silicon is the second most abundant element in the Earth's crust and is vital for the technology industry. It is used to create semiconductors and integrated circuits found in electronic devices.

The Discovery of Phosphorus: Phosphorus was the first element to be discovered that was not known since ancient times. It was isolated in 1669 by Hennig Brand, a German merchant, by boiling urine.

Buckyballs and Nanotechnology: Buckminsterfullerene, or buckyballs, are molecules composed entirely of carbon, shaped like a hollow sphere. They represent a major area of research in nanotechnology.

Platinum's Resistance to Corrosion: Platinum is highly resistant to corrosion and oxidation, making it valuable for various industrial applications, including in catalytic converters in vehicles.

The Versatility of Nitrogen: Nitrogen, making up about 78% of the Earth's atmosphere, is essential for life. It is a key component of amino acids, which are the building blocks of proteins.

Lithium in Batteries: Lithium is a light metal used in rechargeable batteries for mobile phones, laptops, and electric vehicles. Its high electrochemical potential makes it extremely efficient for energy storage.

Chlorophyll's Vital Function: Chlorophyll, the green pigment found in plants, is crucial for photosynthesis, allowing plants to absorb energy from light and produce oxygen.

Dinosaurs & Prehistoric Life

Tyrannosaurus Rex's Powerful Bite: The T. rex had one of the strongest bites of any land animal that ever lived. Its bite force is estimated to be about 12,800 pounds, capable of crushing bone.

Dinosaur Colors: Recent advancements, particularly in analyzing fossilized feathers, suggest that some dinosaurs were brightly colored and not just the drab greens and browns we once imagined.

The Long Reign of Dinosaurs: Dinosaurs roamed the Earth for about 165 million years. In contrast, modern humans have been around for approximately 200,000 years.

Velociraptor's Size: Popular movies have depicted Velociraptors as large and formidable predators, but in reality, they were about the size of a turkey.

Feathered Dinosaurs: Many species of dinosaurs, including the well-known Velociraptor, had feathers. This discovery has transformed our understanding of the connection between dinosaurs and birds.

The Largest Dinosaur: Argentinosaurus is currently the largest dinosaur for which there is convincing evidence. It was a massive herbivore, measuring up to 100 feet long and possibly weighing as much as 100 tons.

Dinosaur Extinction: The most widely accepted theory for the extinction of dinosaurs is the impact of a massive asteroid or comet approximately 66 million years ago, creating a global catastrophe that changed the course of life on Earth.

Pterosaurs Weren't Dinosaurs: Often thought of as dinosaurs, pterosaurs were actually flying reptiles that lived during the same period. They were the first vertebrates known to have evolved powered flight.

Complex Social Behavior: Evidence suggests that some

dinosaurs, like the Triceratops and the Velociraptor, may have exhibited complex social behavior, hunting in packs or living in herds.

Prehistoric Megafauna: Alongside dinosaurs, the prehistoric world was home to a variety of other large animals, including the mammoth, saber-toothed cats, and giant ground sloths, which lived after the dinosaurs had gone extinct.

Spinosaurus Aquatic Adaptations: The Spinosaurus is believed to have been semi-aquatic, with physical adaptations for swimming. This sets it apart from most other dinosaur species, which were primarily land-dwelling.

Dinosaur Eggs and Nests: Fossilized dinosaur eggs and nests have been found around the world, providing evidence that some dinosaurs cared for their young after hatching, similar to modern birds.

Massive Herbivores: The Sauropods, including species like Brachiosaurus and Diplodocus, were some of the largest herbivores to walk the Earth. They had long necks and tails, with some reaching lengths over 100 feet.

The First Birds: Archaeopteryx is widely considered the first known bird, living in the Late Jurassic period. It had feathers and wings like modern birds, but also teeth and other dinosaur-like characteristics.

Theropods' Three-Toed Feet: Many theropods, a group of bipedal carnivorous dinosaurs including the T. rex and Velociraptor, had a distinctive three-toed foot structure, leaving a unique footprint that is often found in fossil records.

Stegosaurus' Spiky Tail: The Stegosaurus, known for its row of spinal plates, had a spiky tail it could use as a defensive weapon against predators.

Ankylosaurus Armor: The Ankylosaurus was like a living tank, with a body covered in bony plates and a heavy club-like tail for defense. It was one of the last ankylosaurids to appear before the Cretaceous-Paleogene extinction event.

Continental Drift and Dinosaur Distribution: The movement of Earth's continents affected the evolution and spread of dinosaurs. The supercontinent Pangaea began to break apart during the Mesozoic era, leading to isolated evolution and diverse dinosaur fauna on different continents.

Oviraptor Misunderstanding: The Oviraptor, initially believed to be an egg thief due to the discovery of its fossils near a nest, is now thought to have been a caring parent that was guarding its own eggs.

Giganotosaurus vs. T. rex: The Giganotosaurus, which lived during the Late Cretaceous period in what is now Argentina, was one of the largest meat-eating dinosaurs, slightly larger than the T. rex, though it's unclear if they were more powerful.

World Religions and Mythologies

Hinduism's Pantheon: Hinduism has one of the most complex pantheons in world religions, with over 33 million gods and goddesses. These deities represent various aspects of life and the universe.

Buddhism's Spread Without Conquest: Buddhism is unique among major world religions as it spread across Asia mostly through peaceful means like trade and missionary work, rather than military conquest.

Ancient Greek Mythology's Influence: Ancient Greek mythology has profoundly influenced Western culture, art, and literature. Many contemporary words, phrases, and expressions in Western languages are derived from it.

Norse Mythology and Days of the Week: Several days of the week in English are named after Norse gods and celestial bodies. For example, Thursday is named after Thor, the god of thunder.

Christianity's Early Symbols: Before the cross, early Christians used a variety of symbols, including the ichthys (fish) and the anchor. The fish symbol was a secret sign used to identify fellow believers.

Judaism's Kabbalah: Kabbalah is a mystical aspect of Judaism. It explores esoteric teachings about God, the universe, and the nature of the soul, and has influenced various philosophies and literary works.

Islam's Contributions to Science and Culture: During the Golden Age of Islam (8th to 14th centuries), Islamic scholars made significant advances in fields like mathematics, astronomy, medicine, and literature.

Egyptian Mythology's Afterlife: Ancient Egyptians believed in a complex afterlife, involving a journey to the underworld and a judgment by Osiris. The heart was weighed against the feather of Ma'at (truth) to determine the soul's fate.

Shinto and Natural Elements: Shinto, an indigenous religion of Japan, centers around kami, spirits associated with natural elements and ancestors. It emphasizes harmony with nature and rituals to keep away evil spirits.

Taoism's Yin and Yang: In Taoism, the concept of yin and yang represents dualities in the universe, such as light and dark, fire and water, and male and female. These forces are seen as interconnected and complementary.

Aztec Mythology: The Aztecs had a rich pantheon of gods and goddesses, with Huitzilopochtli, the god of sun and war, being one of the most prominent. They practiced human sacrifices to ensure the sun would rise each day.

African Mythologies: Africa's diverse cultures have a rich tapestry of mythologies, often centered around earth and ancestor spirits. Many African myths explain natural phenomena and teach moral lessons.

Sikhism's Holy Scripture: The Guru Granth Sahib, the holy scripture of Sikhism, is unique among major religious texts as it is written in verse and contains writings by the religion's ten Gurus as well as Hindu and Muslim saints.

Native American Totem Poles: In some Native American cultures, totem poles are a form of storytelling, with carvings representing and recounting family lineages, legends, and notable events.

Zoroastrianism's Influence: One of the world's oldest monotheistic religions, Zoroastrianism, is thought to have significantly influenced other major world religions, including Judaism, Christianity, and Islam.

Hawaiian Mythology: Hawaiian mythology is rich with tales of gods, goddesses, and heroes. Pele, the goddess of volcanoes and fire, is one of the most well-known figures and is believed to reside in the Kilauea volcano.

Confucianism's Impact on East Asia: Confucianism, founded by Confucius, is not just a religion but a philosophical and ethical system that has had a profound influence on the culture, social structures, and governments of East Asian countries.

Roman Mythology and Governance: Roman mythology, heavily influenced by Greek mythology, was deeply intertwined with the Roman state religion. Many Roman emperors were deified and worshipped after their deaths.

Celtic Mythology and Art: Celtic mythology, known for its vivid tales of gods, heroes, and mystical creatures, has also significantly influenced Celtic art, which is famous for its intricate, interwoven patterns and symbolism.

The Jataka Tales in Buddhism: The Jataka tales are a voluminous body of literature concerning the previous births of Gautama Buddha. These stories teach moral lessons and are important in Buddhist culture.

Art Movements & Styles

Impressionism: Originating in the late 19th century, Impressionism was characterized by a focus on light and its changing qualities, often with thin brush strokes and an emphasis on the depiction of natural elements. It was initially criticized for its unfinished and sketch-like appearance.

Cubism: Pioneered by Pablo Picasso and Georges Braque,

Cubism broke away from traditional art by depicting subjects from multiple perspectives simultaneously, creating a fragmented and abstracted form.

Surrealism: Emerging in the early 20th century, Surrealism sought to release the creative potential of the unconscious mind. Artists like Salvador Dalí created bizarre, dream-like images that challenged viewers' perceptions of reality.

Abstract Expressionism: This post-World War II art movement, centered in New York City, was characterized by gestural brush-strokes or mark-making and the impression of spontaneity. Jackson Pollock's drip paintings are iconic of this movement.

Pop Art: Emerging in the 1950s, Pop Art challenged traditional fine art by incorporating imagery from popular and mass culture, such as advertising, comic books, and mundane cultural objects. Andy Warhol and Roy Lichtenstein were key figures in this movement.

Renaissance: The Renaissance was a period of great cultural change and achievement, originating in Italy during the 14th century. It is marked by a revival of classical learning, with artists like Leonardo da Vinci and Michelangelo emphasizing realism and humanism.

Baroque: This style emerged in the early 17th century and is characterized by exaggerated motion, clear detail, and easily interpreted symbolism to produce drama, tension, and grandeur. Caravaggio and Rembrandt are notable Baroque artists.

Dadaism: Developed in reaction to World War I, Dadaism involved visual arts, literature, poetry, art manifestoes, and theatre. It was anti-war, anti-bourgeois, and had political affinities with the radical left.

Fauvism: This style of painting, developed in France at the beginning of the 20th century, is distinguished by strong colors and fierce brushwork. Henri Matisse was a leading figure in this movement.

Art Deco: Popular in the 1920s and 1930s, Art Deco is an eclectic style that combines traditional craft motifs with Machine Age imagery and materials. It is characterized by its bold geometric shapes and lavish ornamentation.

Pre-Raphaelite Brotherhood: Formed in 1848 in England, the Pre-Raphaelite Brotherhood rebelled against the mainstream academic painting. They sought a return to the abundant detail, intense colors, and complex compositions of Quattrocento Italian art.

Art Nouveau: Emerging in the late 19th century, Art Nouveau was known for its flowing, curvilinear designs inspired by natural forms. It encompassed a variety of arts and crafts, including architecture, furniture, and graphic design. The movement is exemplified by the works of Alphonse Mucha and the architecture of Antoni Gaudí.

Futurism: This early 20th-century Italian movement celebrated modernity, technology, and speed. Futurist artists like Umberto Boccioni and Giacomo Balla attempted to capture the dynamism and energy of the modern world in their work.

Constructivism: Originating in Russia around 1913, Constructivism was an artistic and architectural philosophy that rejected the idea of autonomous art in favor of art as a practice directed towards social purposes. Its geometric abstraction influenced modern architecture and design.

De Stijl: Founded in the Netherlands in 1917, De Stijl (The Style) was an art movement advocating pure abstraction and simplicity – form reduced to the essentials of geometric forms and primary colors. Piet Mondrian was a prominent figure in this movement.

Op Art: Short for Optical Art, this visual art style uses optical illusions and was prominent in the 1960s. Artists like Bridget Riley created works that give the viewer the impression of movement, flashing, vibrating patterns, or swelling or warping.

Bauhaus: The Bauhaus was a German art school operational from 1919 to 1933 that combined crafts and the fine arts. Its approach to design influenced modernist architecture and is noted for its functional forms and clean lines.

The Harlem Renaissance: This cultural movement of the 1920s and 1930s centered in Harlem, New York, witnessed an explosion of African-American art, music, and literature. It reshaped African-American identity and history and influenced future generations of Black artists.

Symbolism: In the late 19th century, Symbolism emerged as a reaction against Realism and Impressionism. Artists like

Gustav Klimt and Edvard Munch conveyed emotional experience rather than physical reality, often focusing on dreams, myth, and spirituality.

Minimalism: Developed in the late 1950s and 1960s, Minimalism is an art movement that emphasizes extreme simplification of form and color. Artists like Donald Judd and Agnes Martin sought to strip art down to its essential qualities.

Musical Instruments & Genres

The Stradivarius Mystique: Stradivarius violins, crafted by Antonio Stradivari in the 17th and 18th centuries, are renowned for their unmatched sound quality. The secret behind their exceptional sound remains a mystery and a subject of much speculation.

The Evolution of the Piano: The piano, invented by

Bartolomeo Cristofori in the early 18th century, evolved from earlier instruments like the harpsichord and clavichord. Unlike its predecessors, the piano allows for dynamic control of volume based on the player's touch.

TSaxophone's Invention for Jazz: The saxophone was invented in 1846 by Adolphe Sax, a Belgian instrument maker. While initially used in military bands, it became a key instrument in jazz music in the early 20th century.

Guitar's Ancient Roots: The modern guitar has ancient roots, with similar instruments appearing in ancient civilizations like Egypt and Rome. The six-string version we know today became popular in the 19th century.

Theremin's Electronic Oddity: The theremin, one of the first electronic instruments, is unique because it is played without physical contact. It was invented in 1920 by Russian inventor Léon Theremin.

Drums as Communication Tools: In various cultures, drums were used not just for music but also as a means of communication. African talking drums, for example, could mimic the tones of a spoken language and send complex messages over long distances.

The Versatility of the Violin: The violin is a versatile instrument used in many musical genres, from classical and folk to rock and jazz. It has four strings and can produce a wide range of sounds and tones.

Jazz's Improvisational Brilliance: Jazz, originating in the late 19th to early 20th century, is notable for its emphasis on improvisation, syncopated rhythms, and the use of blue notes.

Rock Music's Cultural Revolution: Emerging in the 1950s, rock music became a symbol of cultural and social revolution. It has since branched into various sub-genres, each with its own distinct style and cultural impact.

The Global Influence of Electronic Music: Electronic music, born from the development of electronic musical instruments and technology, has become one of the most popular and diverse genres globally, influencing various aspects of culture and entertainment.

Bagpipes' Diverse Origins: Often associated with Scotland, bagpipes have a history that spans across many cultures and countries, including Ireland, Spain, and parts of the Middle East, dating back thousands of years.

The Didgeridoo's Ancient Roots: The didgeridoo, traditionally used by indigenous Australians, is one of the world's oldest wind instruments. It's believed to date back over 1,000 years and is known for its distinctive, deep drone.

The Oud's Influence: The oud, a lute-like stringed instrument prominent in Middle Eastern music, is believed to have influenced the development of the European lute, which in turn led to the modern guitar.

Reggae's Social Message: Originating in Jamaica in the 1960s, reggae music is not just known for its unique rhythm and sound but also for conveying messages of peace, love, and social protest.

The Accordion's Versatility: The accordion, developed in the early 19th century, plays a crucial role in various music genres worldwide, from European folk and classical music to American Zydeco and South American tango.

Opera's Dramatic Storytelling: Opera, a key part of Western classical music tradition, originated in Italy at the end of the 16th century. It combines music, drama, stage design, and costumes to tell a story, often with elaborate and theatrical presentations.

The Sitar's Resonance in Psychedelic Rock: The sitar, a classical Indian stringed instrument, gained popularity in Western music in the 1960s. It was famously used by The Beatles, influencing the sound of psychedelic rock.

Blues Music's Roots in African-American History: Blues music, originating in the American Deep South in the late 19th century, has its roots in African-American work songs, spirituals, and folk music. It's known for its distinct use of the blue note and narrative style.

Country Music's Storytelling: Emerging in the Southern United States in the 1920s, country music is characterized by its straightforward, narrative style, often reflecting the everyday life and struggles of American rural folk.

The Theremin's Sci-Fi Association: Besides being one of the first electronic instruments, the theremin became popularly associated with science fiction movies in the 1950s and 1960s due to its eerie, wavering sound.

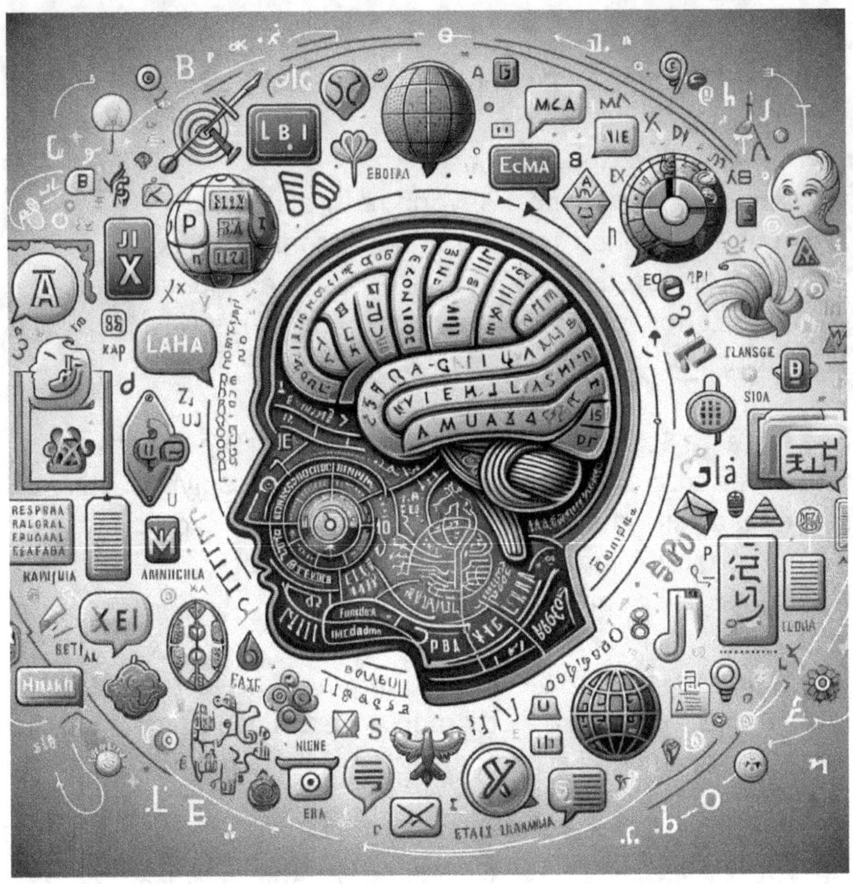

Languages & Linguistics

Thousands of Languages: There are approximately 7,000 languages spoken around the world today. However, many of them are in danger of extinction, with a language dying approximately every two weeks.

Papua New Guinea's Linguistic Diversity: Papua New Guinea is the most linguistically diverse country in the world, with over 800 languages spoken, which is about 12% of the world's total.

Constructed Languages: Beyond natural languages, there are numerous constructed languages (conlangs), like Esperanto, created with the hope of fostering international communication, or Klingon from the Star Trek series, created for artistic purposes.

The Rosetta Stone's Key to Decipherment: The Rosetta Stone was crucial in deciphering Egyptian hieroglyphs. The stone features a decree in three scripts – hieroglyphic, Demotic, and Ancient Greek – allowing scholars to unlock the language of ancient Egypt.

Language Families: The world's languages are categorized into families that share a common ancestral language. The Indo-European family is the largest, including languages like English, Spanish, Russian, and Hindi.

Unique Writing Systems: While many languages use alphabets, others use different writing systems. For example, Chinese characters are logograms, and Arabic and Hebrew are written in abjads, where only consonants are typically written.

The Sumerian Language: Sumerian, spoken in ancient Mesopotamia, is one of the oldest known written languages, dating back to at least 3500 BC.

Languages Without Words for Numbers: Some Amazonian languages, like Pirahã, reportedly have no fixed words for numbers and very few terms for quantifying objects.

Whistled Languages: Some languages, like Silbo Gomero in the Canary Islands and Kuş Dili in Turkey, are whistled rather than spoken, allowing communication over long distances.

Chomsky's Universal Grammar: Linguist Noam Chomsky proposed the theory of Universal Grammar, suggesting that the ability to acquire language is innate to humans and that all human languages share a common structural basis.

Dialects vs. Languages: The distinction between a dialect and a language can be subjective and often influenced by political or cultural factors. A famous saying, attributed to linguist Max Weinreich, is "a language is a dialect with an army and navy."

The Basque Language's Mystery: The Basque language, or Euskara, spoken in the Basque Country in Spain and France, is a linguistic enigma. It is a language isolate, meaning it has no known relation to any other language family in the world.

Endangered Languages: It is estimated that one language becomes extinct every 14 days. When a language dies, the world loses a unique perspective and a wealth of traditional knowledge.

Sanskrit's Complexity: Sanskrit, an ancient Indian language, is known for its complex grammar and precise phonetics. It has significantly influenced many modern languages of the Indian subcontinent.

Linguistic Relativity: The Sapir-Whorf hypothesis, or the principle of linguistic relativity, suggests that the structure of a language affects its speakers' world view or cognition.

The Longest Word: The longest word in the Oxford English Dictionary is 'pneumonoultramicroscopicsilicovolcanoconiosis', a lung disease caused by inhaling very fine ash and sand dust. However, this word was coined to be deliberately long.

Sign Languages' Diversity: There are over 300 different sign languages used around the world. Like spoken languages, they have their own syntax, grammar, and regional dialects.

Tonal Languages: In tonal languages, like Mandarin Chinese and Thai, the meaning of a word changes with the pitch or tone in which it is spoken.

Cuneiform Writing: One of the earliest systems of writing, cuneiform, was developed by the Sumerians of ancient Mesopotamia around 3500-3000 BCE. It involved pressing a reed stylus into clay.

The Inuktitut Syllabary: The Inuit people of Northern Canada use a writing system called Inuktitut, which is made up of symbols representing syllables. It's a unique example of a syllabary developed in the 20th century.

Modern Technologies & AI

Quantum Computing: Quantum computers operate on the principles of quantum mechanics and have the potential to solve complex problems much faster than classical computers. They use quantum bits or qubits, which can exist in multiple states simultaneously.

AI in Healthcare: AI technologies are revolutionizing

healthcare, from diagnosing diseases more accurately and quickly than human practitioners to developing personalized medicine and robotic surgeries.

The Internet of Things (IoT): IoT connects everyday objects to the internet, allowing them to send and receive data. This has applications in various fields, from smart home devices to industrial automation and healthcare monitoring.

5G Technology: The fifth generation of cellular network technology, 5G, promises much faster data download and upload speeds, wider coverage, and more stable connections. It's set to enable innovations like smart cities and autonomous vehicles.

Blockchain Beyond Cryptocurrencies: While blockchain technology is known for its use in cryptocurrencies like Bitcoin, it has potential applications in areas like supply chain management, voting systems, and secure data sharing.

CRISPR Gene Editing: CRISPR-Cas9 is a revolutionary gene-editing technology that allows for precise, directed changes to genomic DNA. It has significant implications for the treatment of genetic disorders, agriculture, and even biofuel production.

Augmented Reality (AR) and Virtual Reality (VR): AR and VR technologies are not just for gaming; they're used in education, training simulations, healthcare, interior design, and retail.

Artificial Photosynthesis: Scientists are developing systems that mimic photosynthesis to capture carbon dioxide and sunlight, producing organic compounds and, potentially, renewable energy sources.

Autonomous Vehicles: Self-driving cars use AI, sensors, and advanced algorithms to navigate and make decisions. This technology could revolutionize transportation, reducing accidents and improving traffic management.

Nanotechnology: Nanotech involves manipulating matter at an atomic or molecular scale. It has wide-ranging applications, from creating new materials and devices in medicine, electronics, biomaterials, and energy production.

Sophisticated AI Algorithms: AI algorithms have become so advanced that they can write articles, compose music, create art, and even generate new AI algorithms. This capability is expanding the boundaries of creativity and efficiency.

The Rise of Edge Computing: Edge computing brings computation and data storage closer to the location where it is needed, improving response times and saving bandwidth. It's crucial for technologies like IoT and self-driving cars.

Advances in Battery Technology: Modern research in battery technology focuses on making batteries more efficient, durable, and environmentally friendly. Innovations include solid-state batteries, which promise higher energy density and safety compared to traditional lithium-ion batteries.

Biometrics in Security: Biometric technology uses unique human characteristics, such as fingerprints, facial recognition, or iris scans, for identification and access control. It's becoming increasingly common in devices like smartphones and security systems.

3D Printing Evolution: 3D printing has evolved beyond plastics to include a variety of materials, including metal, glass, and even human tissue. This technology is revolutionizing manufacturing, healthcare, and even space exploration.

Wearable Technology: Wearable devices, such as smartwatches and fitness trackers, have become mainstream, providing users with real-time data on their health and fitness, and even allowing remote patient monitoring in healthcare.

Voice Assistants and NLP: Voice assistants like Amazon's Alexa, Apple's Siri, and Google Assistant have become household technologies, advancing natural language processing (NLP) capabilities and making human-machine interactions more intuitive.

Neural Networks and Deep Learning: Neural networks, modeled after the human brain, are at the heart of many AI breakthroughs. Deep learning, a subset of machine learning, uses these networks to analyze large sets of data, recognize patterns, and make decisions.

Renewable Energy Technologies: Innovations in solar panels, wind turbines, and other renewable energy technologies are driving the transition towards a more sustainable and cleaner energy future.

Smart Cities: The concept of smart cities utilizes a variety of IoT sensors and technologies to manage assets, resources, and services efficiently. This includes everything from traffic and transportation systems to water supply networks and waste management.

Cultural Festivals & Traditions

India's Holi Festival: Known as the "Festival of Colors," Holi is a Hindu festival celebrating spring, love, and new life. Participants throw colored powder and water at each other, making for a vibrant and joyful celebration.

Chinese New Year: Also known as the Spring Festival, it marks the beginning of the lunar new year. Each year is represented by one of the 12 animals in the Chinese zodiac, and the festival is celebrated with fireworks, dragon dances, and special meals.

Brazil's Carnival: This world-famous festival held before Lent features parades, music, dancing, and elaborate costumes. It's a major event in Brazilian culture, showcasing the country's love for music and dance.

Spain's La Tomatina: Held in the town of Buñol, La Tomatina is a tomato-throwing festival where thousands of participants throw overripe tomatoes at each other, creating a red, messy spectacle.

Japan's Hanami: Hanami, or "flower viewing," is the Japanese tradition of enjoying the transient beauty of flowers, particularly cherry blossoms (sakura). It involves outdoor parties under cherry blossom trees during their brief blooming period.

Germany's Oktoberfest: Originating in Munich, Oktoberfest is the world's largest beer festival. Visitors enjoy a wide variety of beers, traditional foods, and fairground attractions.

Diwali, the Festival of Lights: Celebrated by Hindus, Sikhs, and Jains worldwide, Diwali symbolizes the spiritual victory of light over darkness. It's marked by lighting lamps, fireworks, and sharing sweets.

Mexico's Day of the Dead: Día de los Muertos is a celebration of life and death. Families create ofrendas (altars) to honor their deceased loved ones, adorned with marigolds, photographs, and favorite foods of the departed.

Albuquerque International Balloon Fiesta: Held in Albuquerque, New Mexico, this annual festival features over 500 hot air balloons, making it the largest balloon event in the world.

Thailand's Songkran Water Festival: Marking the Thai New Year, Songkran is famous for its massive water fights, symbolizing the washing away of sins and bad luck. It's a time for cleansing, renewal, and fun.

The Lantern Festival in China: Concluding the Chinese New Year celebrations, the Lantern Festival features night-time displays of thousands of lanterns. It's also associated with matchmaking activities and traditional dances like the lion dance.

Mardi Gras in New Orleans: Mardi Gras, or Fat Tuesday, is celebrated with parades, masquerade balls, and king cakes in New Orleans, Louisiana. It marks the last day of feasting before the Lenten season in Christian traditions.

The Running of the Bulls in Spain: Part of the San Fermín festival in Pamplona, this event involves running in front of a small group of bulls that have been let loose on the city's streets. It's a tradition that dates back to the 14th century.

Kumbh Mela in India: One of the largest religious gatherings in the world, the Kumbh Mela is a Hindu pilgrimage which rotates among four sacred rivers. Devotees believe that bathing in these rivers during the festival cleanses them of their sins.

Balinese Nyepi Day: Nyepi, the Balinese Day of Silence, is marked by a day of fasting, meditation, and self-reflection. The entire island of Bali shuts down, including the airport, and tourists are encouraged to stay indoors.

The Edinburgh Festival Fringe in Scotland: The world's largest arts festival, it takes place every August for three weeks in Edinburgh. It's an open-access festival where artists can perform regardless of their professional or amateur status.

The Calgary Stampede in Canada: Known as "The Greatest Outdoor Show on Earth," the Calgary Stampede is a ten-day event featuring a large parade, world-class rodeo, concerts, and cultural exhibitions.

Loi Krathong in Thailand: Celebrated annually throughout Thailand, Loi Krathong involves floating a krathong (a small raft made from banana leaves and flowers) on a river. This act is meant to honor the water spirits and wash away bad luck.

Carnival of Venice in Italy: Famous for its elaborate masks and costumes, the Carnival of Venice is one of the oldest festivals in the world. It's a celebration of the end of Lent, filled with balls, parades, and music.

White Nights Festival in Russia: Held during the season of the midnight sun in St. Petersburg, this festival features classical ballet, opera, and music events, culminating in the Scarlet Sails celebration, a massive show with fireworks and a water parade.

Famous Architectural Wonders

The Great Wall of China: Spanning over 13,000 miles, the Great Wall is not a single wall but a series of walls and fortifications. It was built over several centuries, starting as early as the 7th century BC, to protect against invasions.

The Eiffel Tower in Paris: Originally a temporary structure built for the 1889 World's Fair, the Eiffel Tower has become a global icon of France and a symbol of romance. It's about 1,063 feet tall, roughly equivalent to an 81-story building.

The Taj Mahal's Love Story: Located in Agra, India, the Taj Mahal was built by Mughal Emperor Shah Jahan in memory of his beloved wife Mumtaz Mahal. This white marble mausoleum is an outstanding example of Mughal architecture and is a UNESCO World Heritage Site.

The Engineering of the Pyramids of Giza: The largest, the Great Pyramid, was originally 481 feet tall and consisted of 2.3 million stone blocks, each weighing an average of 2.5 to 15 tons. How the ancient Egyptians built these structures remains a topic of debate.

The Colosseum's Ancient Spectacles: In Rome, the Colosseum could hold up to 80,000 spectators and was used for gladiatorial contests and public spectacles such as mock sea battles, animal hunts, and executions.

Petra's Rock-Cut Architecture: The ancient city of Petra in Jordan, famous for its rock-cut architecture and water conduit system, is also known as the "Rose City" due to the color of the stone from which it is carved.

The Leaning Tower of Pisa's Inclination: This tower in Italy is famous for its unintended tilt. Construction began in the 12th century, but the foundation was built on soft ground, causing the tilt. Efforts to stabilize it have been ongoing.

Machu Picchu's Incan Mystery: Located in the Andes Mountains of Peru, Machu Picchu is an Incan citadel believed to be constructed in the 15th century. Its exact purpose remains unknown, but it's one of the most iconic symbols of the Inca Empire.

The Sydney Opera House's Unique Design: In Australia, the Sydney Opera House's design was so innovative that its construction posed a great challenge. The distinctive sail-like shells were a revolutionary design when it was opened in 1973.

Angkor Wat's Religious Shift: Originally built as a Hindu temple dedicated to the god Vishnu in the early 12th century, Angkor Wat in Cambodia gradually transformed into a Buddhist temple by the end of the 12th century.

Sagrada Família's Ongoing Construction: The Basílica de la Sagrada Família in Barcelona, designed by Antoni Gaudí, has been under construction since 1882. Its intricate design and detailed symbolism make it one of the most unique and studied architectural projects in the world.

Burj Khalifa's Record Height: Standing at 2,717 feet, the Burj Khalifa in Dubai is the tallest building in the world. It's a marvel of modern engineering and is designed to resemble the shape of a desert flower.

The Forbidden City's Scale: In Beijing, the Forbidden City is a massive palace complex that served as the home of emperors for nearly 500 years. It consists of 980 buildings and covers 180 acres, making it the largest palace complex in the world.

St. Peter's Basilica's Artistic Contribution: Located in Vatican City, St. Peter's Basilica is one of the largest churches in the world and a renowned example of Renaissance architecture. It houses works by artists like Michelangelo and

Bernini.

The Chrysler Building's Art Deco Style: This building in New York City is a classic example of Art Deco architecture. When it was completed in 1930, it was the world's tallest building before being surpassed by the Empire State Building.

Stonehenge's Mystery: Located in England, Stonehenge is a prehistoric monument whose purpose remains a topic of debate. It consists of a ring of standing stones, each around 13 feet high and weighing about 25 tons.

Guggenheim Museum Bilbao's Innovative Design: Designed by Frank Gehry, this museum in Spain is noted for its innovative design, featuring titanium curves and shapes that change appearance with the light.

Neuschwanstein Castle's Fairy Tale Look: In Germany, Neuschwanstein Castle was the inspiration for Disney's Sleeping Beauty Castle. Built in the 19th century, it's known for its romantic architecture and picturesque setting.

The Lotus Temple's Flower Shape: The Lotus Temple in New Delhi, India, is a Bahá'í House of Worship notable for its flowerlike shape. It has won numerous architectural awards and is open to people of all religions.

The Hoover Dam's Engineering Feat: This dam on the border between Arizona and Nevada was an engineering marvel of its time. Completed in 1936, it created one of the largest man-made lakes in the world, Lake Mead.

Sport & Olympic Games

Usain Bolt's Unmatched Speed: Jamaican sprinter Usain Bolt is widely considered the greatest sprinter of all time. He holds world records in the 100 meters, 200 meters, and 4 × 100 meters relay, and is an eight-time Olympic gold medalist.

Michael Phelps' Record Medals: American swimmer Michael Phelps is the most decorated Olympian of all time, with a total of 28 medals, including 23 gold medals. His incredible performance in the 2008 Beijing Olympics, where he won eight gold medals, remains unmatched.

The Ancient Olympic Games: The original Olympic Games were held in Olympia, Greece, from the 8th century BC to the 4th century AD. Unlike the modern Olympics, the ancient games were a religious festival in honor of Zeus.

Nadia Comăneci's Perfect 10: At the 1976 Montreal Olympics, Romanian gymnast Nadia Comăneci became the first gymnast to score a perfect 10 in an Olympic gymnastics event. She was only 14 years old at the time.

Jesse Owens' 1936 Berlin Triumph: American track and field athlete Jesse Owens won four gold medals in the 1936 Berlin Olympics, a remarkable achievement that was seen as a powerful statement against Nazi ideology.

The Marathon's Origin: The marathon race was inspired by the legend of Pheidippides, a Greek messenger who ran from the Battle of Marathon to Athens to announce the Greek victory over Persia. The distance of the modern marathon was standardized at 26.2 miles in 1921.

The First Winter Olympics: The first Winter Olympic Games were held in Chamonix, France, in 1924. Initially called "International Winter Sports Week," it was retroactively named the first Winter Olympics.

Women in the Olympics: Women first competed in the Olympics in the 1900 Paris Games in tennis and golf. The range of women's events has since expanded dramatically, with women's boxing added as recently as 2012.

The Paralympic Games: Established in 1960, the Paralympic Games are a major international multi-sport event for athletes with disabilities. They emphasize the participants' athletic achievements rather than their disability.

The Olympic Torch Relay: The tradition of the Olympic torch relay started in 1936 for the Berlin Games. The flame is lit at the site of the ancient Olympics in Olympia, Greece, and then carried to the host country, symbolizing the connection between the ancient and modern games.

Bob Beamon's Long Jump Record: During the 1968 Mexico City Olympics, American athlete Bob Beamon set a long jump world record of 29 feet and 2.5 inches (8.90 meters), a record that stood for 23 years and is still the Olympic record.

The Introduction of Basketball: Basketball made its Olympic debut at the 1936 Berlin Games. Interestingly, the sport was played outdoors on a dirt court, and the USA won the first gold medal in the sport.

Simone Biles' Gymnastics Dominance: American gymnast Simone Biles, considered one of the greatest gymnasts of all time, has won a combined total of 30 Olympic and World Championship medals. She is renowned for her athleticism and has several gymnastics skills named after her.

The Miracle on Ice: During the 1980 Winter Olympics in Lake Placid, the USA ice hockey team, composed of amateur players, defeated the Soviet Union team, who were considered the best in the world, in an event known as the "Miracle on Ice."

Fencer Ibtihaj Muhammad's Barrier-Breaking Moment: At the 2016 Rio Olympics, Ibtihaj Muhammad became the first American athlete to compete in the Olympics wearing a hijab. She was part of the USA team that won a bronze medal in team sabre.

Sir Steve Redgrave's Rowing Achievements: British rower Sir Steve Redgrave won gold medals in five consecutive Olympic Games from 1984 to 2000, making him one of the most successful rowers in Olympic history.

The Four-minute Mile: Roger Bannister, a British athlete, broke the four-minute barrier in the mile run in 1954, a feat that was considered impossible at the time. His record-breaking time was 3 minutes and 59.4 seconds.

Cathy Freeman's Iconic Win: Australian sprinter Cathy Freeman won the 400 meters at the 2000 Sydney Olympics, becoming the first Aboriginal person to win an individual Olympic gold medal. Her victory was celebrated as a moment of national unity.

The Iron War at the Hawaii Ironman: In 1989, the Ironman World Championship in Hawaii witnessed one of the most famous duels in triathlon history. Mark Allen and Dave Scott battled side by side for the majority of the race, with Allen eventually winning.

The FIFA World Cup's Global Appeal: The FIFA World Cup, first held in 1930, is the most prestigious soccer tournament in the world and is watched by billions of people globally. The 1950 World Cup match between Brazil and Uruguay holds the record for the highest attendance in a soccer match, with over

199,000 spectators.

Mathematical Concepts & Theories

Pythagoras and His Theorem: Pythagoras, an ancient Greek mathematician, is best known for the Pythagorean Theorem. The theorem, which states that in a right-angled triangle, the square of the hypotenuse is equal to the sum of the squares of the other two sides, is a fundamental principle in geometry.

The Story of Zero: The concept of zero as a number was

revolutionary in the history of mathematics. It originated in India around the 5th century and was later developed in the 7th century by the Indian mathematician Brahmagupta.

Archimedes' Eureka Moment: The Greek mathematician Archimedes reportedly exclaimed "Eureka!" (I have found it!) when he stepped into a bath and noticed the water level rise, leading him to understand the concept of volume displacement.

The Invention of Calculus: Calculus, a major branch of mathematics, was developed independently in the late 17th century by Isaac Newton and Gottfried Wilhelm Leibniz. Their formulations are the foundation of many areas of modern science and engineering.

Euler's Identity: Considered by many as the most beautiful theorem in mathematics, Euler's Identity ($e^{\pi i} + 1 = 0$) combines five fundamental mathematical constants in a surprisingly simple and elegant way.

The Enigma Machine and Alan Turing: Mathematician Alan Turing played a crucial role in World War II by developing techniques for breaking German ciphers, particularly the Enigma code, significantly impacting the course of the war.

The Mystery of Prime Numbers: Prime numbers, integers greater than 1 that have no divisors other than 1 and themselves, have fascinated mathematicians for centuries. The distribution of primes remains one of the great unsolved problems in mathematics.

Sophie Germain's Contributions: Despite facing gender

barriers, 19th-century French mathematician Sophie Germain made significant contributions to number theory and the theory of elasticity. Her work laid the groundwork for modern theories in both fields.

Fibonacci Sequence in Nature: The Fibonacci sequence, where each number is the sum of the two preceding ones, appears frequently in nature, from the arrangement of leaves on a stem to the pattern of seeds in a sunflower.

Poincaré Conjecture: Solved in 2003 by Russian mathematician Grigori Perelman, the Poincaré Conjecture was one of the most famous unsolved problems in topology, a branch of mathematics concerned with the properties of space that are preserved under continuous transformations.

Andrew Wiles and Fermat's Last Theorem: British mathematician Andrew Wiles famously proved Fermat's Last Theorem in 1994, a problem that had remained unsolved for over 350 years since it was first conjectured by Pierre de Fermat in 1637.

The Beauty of the Mandelbrot Set: Discovered by Benoit Mandelbrot in 1980, the Mandelbrot Set is a set of complex numbers that produces a fractal, a never-ending pattern that is self-similar across different scales. It's known for its captivating and intricate shapes.

Hypatia of Alexandria: Hypatia was a renowned mathematician, astronomer, and philosopher in ancient Alexandria. She is one of the first female mathematicians whose life and work are well recorded.

Non-Euclidean Geometry: The development of non-Euclidean geometry by mathematicians like Nikolai Lobachevsky and János Bolyai in the 19th century revolutionized the field, challenging long-held assumptions about space and laying groundwork for Einstein's theory of general relativity.

The Four Color Theorem: This theorem states that no more than four colors are needed to color the regions of a map so that no two adjacent regions have the same color. It was the first major theorem to be proven using a computer.

Ramanujan's Mathematical Genius: Indian mathematician Srinivasa Ramanujan, largely self-taught, made extraordinary contributions to mathematical analysis, number theory, infinite series, and continued fractions.

The Millennium Prize Problems: These are seven problems in mathematics that were stated by the Clay Mathematics Institute in 2000. Solving any one of these unsolved problems results in a prize of one million dollars.

Gödel's Incompleteness Theorems: In 1931, Kurt Gödel published his incompleteness theorems, showing that in any sufficiently powerful mathematical system, there are propositions that cannot be proved or disproved within the system.

The Monty Hall Problem: This probability puzzle, based on a TV game show scenario, became famous after a reader's letter was published in "Parade" magazine in 1990. It demonstrates a counter-intuitive solution that challenges our understanding of probability theory.

The Golden Ratio in Art and Nature: The Golden Ratio, approximately equal to 1.618, has been used in art and architecture for its aesthetically pleasing properties. It also appears in patterns in nature, such as the spirals of shells and the arrangement of leaves.

Environmental Science & Ecology

Rachel Carson and 'Silent Spring': Rachel Carson, a marine biologist and environmentalist, authored "Silent Spring" in 1962, a groundbreaking book that helped launch the modern environmental movement. It focused on the dangers of chemical pesticides to the environment and human health.

The Formation of the EPA: The United States Environmental

Protection Agency (EPA) was established in 1970 following growing public concern about environmental pollution. It was a significant step in government-led environmental protection efforts.

Chernobyl and Environmental Impact: The Chernobyl disaster in 1986 was one of the worst nuclear accidents in history, releasing large amounts of radioactive materials into the environment. The incident has led to ongoing research into the effects of radiation on ecosystems.

The Discovery of the Ozone Hole: In 1985, scientists discovered a hole in the ozone layer over Antarctica, leading to the Montreal Protocol in 1987, an international treaty to phase out substances depleting the ozone layer.

The Great Pacific Garbage Patch: This is a massive area in the Pacific Ocean where a large concentration of plastic waste has accumulated, driven by ocean currents. It highlights the issue of plastic pollution in the world's oceans.

The Introduction of the Concept of Biodiversity: The term 'biodiversity' was first coined in 1985. It encompasses the variety of life on Earth, from genetic and species diversity to the diversity of ecosystems.

The Green Revolution: In the mid-20th century, the Green Revolution introduced new agricultural technologies, including high-yield crop varieties and synthetic fertilizers, significantly increasing food production but also raising concerns about environmental sustainability.

The Keystone Species Concept: Introduced by ecologist

Robert Paine in 1969, the concept of keystone species refers to species that have a disproportionately large impact on their ecosystem relative to their abundance.

Jane Goodall's Chimpanzee Research: Primatologist Jane Goodall's extensive study of chimpanzee social and family life in Gombe Stream National Park revolutionized our understanding of primates and highlighted the importance of conservation.

The Rise of Renewable Energy: Advances in technologies like solar panels, wind turbines, and hydroelectric power are crucial in the global effort to reduce dependence on fossil fuels and combat climate change.

The Blue Carbon Concept: "Blue carbon" refers to carbon captured and stored in coastal and marine ecosystems, primarily mangroves, seagrasses, and salt marshes. These ecosystems are incredibly efficient at storing carbon, making them crucial in combating climate change.

The Impact of Invasive Species: Invasive species, introduced into ecosystems where they are not native, can cause significant ecological disruption. Examples include the zebra mussel in North American lakes and the cane toad in Australia.

The Significance of Coral Reefs: Coral reefs, often called "rainforests of the sea," are some of the most diverse ecosystems on Earth. They provide critical habitats for marine life and offer coastal protection and resources for human communities.

Dian Fossey's Gorilla Research: Dian Fossey, an American primatologist, dedicated her life to studying and protecting mountain gorillas in Rwanda. Her work raised awareness about the species' plight and contributed significantly to gorilla conservation.

The Dust Bowl of the 1930s: This severe dust storm period in North America was caused by extensive farming without crop rotation or other soil conservation techniques. It led to widespread ecological and agricultural damage.

The Creation of National Parks: The establishment of Yellowstone National Park in 1872 marked the beginning of the global national park movement, a crucial step in preserving natural areas for ecological health and public enjoyment.

The Gaia Hypothesis: Proposed by James Lovelock and Lynn Margulis in the 1970s, this hypothesis suggests that Earth functions as a self-regulating system, with life, the atmosphere, the seas, and the earth's crust cooperating to maintain conditions conducive to life.

The Greenhouse Effect Discovery: The greenhouse effect, critical in maintaining Earth's habitable climate, was first proposed by Joseph Fourier in 1824 and later quantified by Svante Arrhenius in the late 19th century.

The Phenomenon of Acid Rain: Identified as a major environmental problem in the 1970s and 1980s, acid rain results from emissions of sulfur dioxide and nitrogen oxide, which react with atmospheric water to produce acids.

The Success of the Endangered Species Act: Enacted in 1973 in the United States, the Endangered Species Act has been instrumental in saving numerous species from extinction, including the bald eagle and the American alligator.

Culinary Delights & Cuisine

The Origin of Pasta: While commonly associated with Italy, pasta's origins might trace back to ancient China. Marco Polo reportedly introduced pasta to Italy from China in the 13th century, although there's evidence that pasta was already known in Italy by then.

French Cuisine's Gastronomic Meals: In 2010, UNESCO

declared French gastronomic meals a "world intangible heritage." French cuisine is known for its emphasis on technique, quality ingredients, and the art of dining.

Sushi's Humble Beginnings: Sushi, now a global phenomenon, originated as a way of preserving fish in fermented rice in Southeast Asia. The sushi we know today, with vinegared rice and fresh fish, developed in Tokyo (formerly Edo) in the early 19th century.

India's Diverse Spices: Indian cuisine is famous for its use of a wide array of spices. Each region in India has its distinct blend of spices and cooking techniques, making its cuisine incredibly diverse.

The Historical Significance of Bread: Bread, one of the oldest prepared foods, has been a staple in many cultures for thousands of years. Ancient Egyptians were the first to bake leavened bread, and it played a significant role in their society and religion.

Chocolate's Preciousness in Mesoamerica: In ancient Mesoamerican cultures, cacao beans were so highly valued that they were used as currency. The chocolate drink was reserved for royalty and religious ceremonies.

The Michelin Guide's Origin: The Michelin Guide, now synonymous with fine dining and gourmet cuisine, was first published in 1900 by the Michelin tire company as a guide to help motorists in France find lodging, food, and gas stations.

Spain's Molecular Gastronomy: Chef Ferran Adrià of El Bulli in Spain revolutionized the culinary world with his approach to molecular gastronomy, using science to create new textures and flavors in food.

Middle Eastern Cuisine's Influence: Middle Eastern cuisine, with its emphasis on spices and herbs like cumin, mint, and saffron, has had a significant influence on European cuisine, particularly through the spice trade.

The Tradition of Dim Sum: Originating in Cantonese cuisine, dim sum involves a variety of small dishes, such as dumplings and buns, traditionally served with tea. The term means "touch the heart," reflecting the small, heartwarming nature of these dishes.

The Evolution of Pizza: Although pizza-like dishes existed in ancient times, the pizza as we know it today originated in Naples, Italy. The classic Margherita pizza was reportedly created in 1889 to honor Queen Margherita of Savoy, featuring tomatoes, mozzarella, and basil to represent the Italian flag's colors.

Turkish Coffee's Cultural Significance: Turkish coffee, known for its strong preparation method and unique serving style, is so culturally important that it was inscribed in UNESCO's Intangible Cultural Heritage List in 2013. Its preparation and consumption are integral to Turkish social customs.

The Origin of Tacos: Tacos, now a staple of Mexican cuisine, were believed to be invented by Mexican silver miners in the 18th century. The word "taco" referred to the little charges they used to excavate the ore.

Japanese Kaiseki Cuisine: Kaiseki is a traditional Japanese multi-course dining experience that emphasizes seasonal ingredients, artful presentation, and a balance of taste, texture, and appearance. It originated from the meals served at tea ceremonies.

The Birth of Caesar Salad: Contrary to popular belief, the Caesar salad was created in Mexico, not Italy. Italian immigrant Caesar Cardini invented it in Tijuana in the 1920s.

The Global Journey of Coffee: Coffee, originally discovered in Ethiopia, made its way to the Middle East in the 15th century, then to Europe in the 17th century, becoming a global commodity. The first European coffee house opened in Venice in 1645.

Thai Cuisine's Balance of Flavors: Thai food is globally renowned for its balance of five fundamental flavors: sweet, spicy, sour, bitter, and salty. Thai cuisine's complexity and harmony of flavors make it distinctively unique.

The Invention of Ice Cream: While frozen desserts have been enjoyed since ancient times, the version of ice cream we know today was likely developed in the 16th century. It's believed that Catherine de Medici introduced it to France when she married the future King Henry II.

The Diversity of Indian Bread: Indian cuisine features an incredible variety of bread, from the well-known naan and roti to regional specialties like Kerala's parotta, Punjab's bhatura, and Gujarat's thepla.

The Cultural Role of Tea in China: In China, tea is more than just a beverage; it's an integral part of the culture. Chinese tea culture includes tea planting, brewing, and elaborate tea ceremonies that focus on the art of tea making.

World Literature & Famous Books

"Don Quixote" and the Birth of the Modern Novel: Written by Miguel de Cervantes and first published in 1605, "Don Quixote" is often considered the first modern novel. It's a landmark in Western literature and a foundational work in the canon.

Shakespeare's Vast Influence: William Shakespeare, often hailed as the greatest writer in the English language, contributed significantly to English literature. His plays and sonnets have shaped the course of drama and poetry and introduced over 1,700 new words to the English language.

The Epic of Gilgamesh: One of the earliest known works of literature, "The Epic of Gilgamesh," dates back to ancient Mesopotamia. This epic poem includes themes of friendship, the quest for fame, and the search for eternal life.

The Gutenberg Bible: The Gutenberg Bible, printed by Johannes Gutenberg in the 1450s, was the first major book printed using movable type in the West. It marked the start of the age of the printed book in the West.

Jane Austen's Timeless Novels: Jane Austen's novels, including "Pride and Prejudice" and "Sense and Sensibility," are celebrated for their wit, social commentary, and insights into the lives of early 19th-century women.

Leo Tolstoy's "War and Peace": Often cited as one of the greatest novels ever written, Tolstoy's "War and Peace" offers a vast panorama of Russian society and a profound meditation on history and human experience.

Gabriel García Márquez's Magical Realism: Colombian author Gabriel García Márquez is renowned for his use of magical realism, a literary style that incorporates magical elements into realistic settings. His novel "One Hundred Years of Solitude" is a landmark in world literature.

The Brontë Sisters' Literary Legacy: Charlotte, Emily, and Anne Brontë, writing under male pseudonyms, made significant contributions to English literature with novels like "Jane Eyre," "Wuthering Heights," and "The Tenant of Wildfell Hall."

"The Tale of Genji": Written by Murasaki Shikibu in the early 11th century, this Japanese work is often considered the world's first novel. It offers a detailed portrayal of court life in medieval Japan.

Homer's "Iliad" and "Odyssey": These ancient Greek epic poems are central works of ancient Greek literature and have had a lasting impact on Western culture, especially their themes of heroism, honor, and the human condition.

Marcel Proust's Monumental Work: French writer Marcel Proust's "In Search of Lost Time" is one of the longest novels ever written, with over a million words. It's renowned for its deep exploration of memory and time.

The Influence of "The Arabian Nights": Also known as "One Thousand and One Nights," this collection of Middle Eastern folk tales has had a profound impact on Western literature and popular culture, introducing stories like "Aladdin's Wonderful Lamp" and "Ali Baba and the Forty Thieves."

Haruki Murakami's Unique Style: Contemporary Japanese author Haruki Murakami is known for his blend of magical realism, surrealism, and melancholy, with popular works like "Norwegian Wood" and "Kafka on the Shore."

Charles Dickens' Social Commentary: British novelist Charles Dickens is celebrated for his vivid characters and depictions of Victorian society. His novels, including "Great Expectations" and "A Tale of Two Cities," often highlighted social injustices of his time.

The Legacy of the Beat Generation: The Beat Generation, a group of American writers in the 1950s, including Jack Kerouac, Allen Ginsberg, and William S. Burroughs, were influential in shaping post-war American literature with their non-conformist attitudes and explorations of American culture.

George Orwell's Dystopian Visions: English novelist George Orwell is famous for his works "1984" and "Animal Farm," which provide critical commentary on totalitarianism, authoritarianism, and the dangers of unchecked political power.

Virginia Woolf's Stream of Consciousness: A key figure in modernist literature, Virginia Woolf, used stream of consciousness as a narrative device to explore the complex inner lives of her characters, as seen in novels like "Mrs. Dalloway" and "To the Lighthouse."

Gabriel Garcia Marquez and Latin American Literature: Gabriel Garcia Marquez's works, including "One Hundred Years of Solitude," were pivotal in bringing Latin American literature to the forefront of the global literary scene, particularly through the style of magical realism.

F. Scott Fitzgerald and the Jazz Age: American author F. Scott Fitzgerald is synonymous with the Jazz Age, capturing the spirit of the 1920s in his works. "The Great Gatsby" remains a poignant exploration of the American Dream.

The Haiku Form in Japanese Poetry: Haiku, a traditional

form of Japanese poetry, consists of three lines with a syllable structure of 5-7-5. Matsuo Basho is one of the most famous poets of this form, known for his concise and evocative descriptions of nature.

Historical Battles & Wars

The Battle of Thermopylae: In 480 BC, the Battle of Thermopylae was fought between an alliance of Greek city-states, led by King Leonidas of Sparta, and the Persian Empire of Xerxes I. Despite being vastly outnumbered, the Greeks held off the Persians for three days in a narrow mountain pass.

Alexander the Great at the Battle of Gaugamela: In 331 BC,

Alexander the Great achieved a decisive victory against the Persian King Darius III. This battle showcased Alexander's tactical brilliance and led to the fall of the Achaemenid Empire.

The Roman Defeat at Teutoburg Forest: In 9 AD, three Roman legions were ambushed and destroyed by Germanic tribes led by Arminius in the Teutoburg Forest. This defeat prevented Roman expansion into Germania.

The Siege of Orleans in the Hundred Years' War: In 1429, during the Hundred Years' War, Joan of Arc played a crucial role in lifting the siege of Orleans by the English, a turning point that led to Charles VII's coronation as the King of France.

The Battle of Waterloo: In 1815, Napoleon Bonaparte's army was defeated at the Battle of Waterloo by the Duke of Wellington, marking the end of Napoleon's rule and the Napoleonic Wars.

The American Civil War's Battle of Gettysburg: In 1863, the Battle of Gettysburg was a turning point in the American Civil War. It was the war's bloodiest battle and ended with General Robert E. Lee's retreat, marking a major victory for the Union.

The Trench Warfare of World War I: World War I saw extensive trench warfare, particularly on the Western Front. The Battle of the Somme in 1916 was one of the largest battles of the war, with over one million casualties.

The Normandy Landings (D-Day): On June 6, 1944, Allied forces conducted a massive amphibious invasion of Normandy, France, marking the beginning of the liberation of Western Europe during World War II.

The Atomic Bombings of Hiroshima and Nagasaki: In August 1945, the United States dropped atomic bombs on the Japanese cities of Hiroshima and Nagasaki, leading to Japan's unconditional surrender and the end of World War II.

The Vietnam War's Tet Offensive: In 1968, the Tet Offensive was a series of surprise attacks by the Viet Cong and North Vietnamese forces against forces of the South Vietnamese Army and the United States. It was a strategic turning point in American public opinion and policy regarding the war.

The Battle of Hastings (1066): This battle saw William the Conqueror defeat King Harold II, leading to the Norman conquest of England. It significantly influenced the English language, culture, and government structure.

Siege of Constantinople (1453): The fall of Constantinople to the Ottoman Empire marked the end of the Byzantine Empire. This event is often cited as the end of the Middle Ages and a pivotal moment leading to the Age of Exploration.

The Spanish Armada (1588): The Spanish Armada's defeat by the English navy was a turning point in naval warfare, marked by the use of more maneuverable and heavily armed English ships, signaling the decline of Spanish maritime dominance.

The Battle of Blenheim (1704): A key battle in the War of Spanish Succession, the Battle of Blenheim was a major victory for the Grand Alliance led by John Churchill, Duke of Marlborough, significantly altering the balance of power in Europe.

The American Revolutionary War's Battle of Saratoga

(1777): Often called the turning point of the American Revolution, the American victory at Saratoga convinced France to enter the war as an ally of the new United States.

The Battle of Trafalgar (1805): Admiral Nelson's naval victory over the combined French and Spanish fleets established British naval supremacy and prevented Napoleon's invasion of Britain.

The American Civil War's Battle of Antietam (1862): Known as the bloodiest single-day battle in American history, Antietam is significant for leading to President Abraham Lincoln's issuance of the Emancipation Proclamation.

The Battle of Verdun (1916): One of the longest and most devastating battles of World War I, the Battle of Verdun lasted about 300 days and resulted in heavy casualties on both French and German sides.

The Six-Day War (1967): A rapid and decisive conflict between Israel and a coalition of Arab states led by Egypt, Syria, and Jordan. The war significantly altered the political landscape of the Middle East.

The Falklands War (1982): This conflict between Argentina and the United Kingdom over the Falkland Islands was notable for being one of the few large-scale naval conflicts since World War II and for the use of modern missile technology in naval warfare.

Psychology & the Human Mind

Sigmund Freud's Psychoanalytic Theory: Freud, often called the father of psychoanalysis, introduced groundbreaking theories about the unconscious mind, the significance of dreams, and the development of personality. His concepts, like the id, ego, and superego, have had a lasting impact on psychology.

Carl Jung and Archetypes: Swiss psychiatrist Carl Jung, a one-time collaborator of Freud, developed analytical psychology. He introduced concepts like the collective unconscious and archetypes, exploring the universal symbols and themes in human psychology.

The Stanford Prison Experiment: Conducted in 1971 by psychologist Philip Zimbardo, this controversial experiment simulated a prison environment to study the effects of perceived power and authority on behavior. The study was criticized for ethical concerns but offered significant insights into human psychology.

The Pavlovian Response: Ivan Pavlov, a Russian physiologist, discovered classical conditioning through his experiments with dogs. He demonstrated how a neutral stimulus, when paired with a significant stimulus, could elicit a conditioned response.

Maslow's Hierarchy of Needs: Abraham Maslow proposed a theory in psychology that human actions are motivated by an innate desire to fulfill needs ranging from the most basic (like food and shelter) to more advanced needs (like esteem and self-actualization).

The Milgram Experiment on Obedience: Stanley Milgram's 1963 experiment tested the extent to which individuals would follow orders from an authority figure, even when the orders involved harming another person. The results raised important ethical and psychological questions about obedience and conscience.

The Myers-Briggs Type Indicator: Developed by Isabel

Briggs Myers and her mother Katharine Cook Briggs, this personality inventory is based on Jungian psychology. It categorizes individuals into 16 personality types based on preferences in how they perceive the world and make decisions.

Elizabeth Loftus and False Memories: Loftus' research on memory has shown that human memory is not only fallible but also malleable. She demonstrated how external suggestions could create false memories, impacting legal and psychological fields.

The Bystander Effect: This social psychological phenomenon, in which individuals are less likely to offer help to a victim when other people are present, was researched extensively following the murder of Kitty Genovese in 1964 in New York City.

Erik Erikson's Stages of Psychosocial Development: Erikson expanded on Freud's theories by emphasizing the importance of social and cultural influences on personality development. He proposed a lifespan model of development, consisting of eight stages from infancy to adulthood.

The Rosenhan Experiment: In a famous 1973 study, psychologist David Rosenhan and others feigned hallucinations to gain admission to psychiatric hospitals. Their experiences revealed significant issues in psychiatric diagnosis and the treatment of mental illness.

B.F. Skinner and Behaviorism: Renowned for his work in behaviorism, B.F. Skinner developed the theory of operant conditioning, demonstrating how behaviors could be shaped by reinforcement or punishment.

Jean Piaget's Theory of Cognitive Development: Piaget's theory revolutionized our understanding of child development by suggesting that children think differently than adults and progress through four stages of cognitive growth.

The Concept of Emotional Intelligence: Popularized by psychologist Daniel Goleman in the 1990s, emotional intelligence (EQ) is the ability to identify, assess, and control one's own emotions, as well as those of others and groups.

Mirror Neurons Discovery: In the 1990s, researchers discovered mirror neurons, which fire both when an individual acts and when the individual observes the same action performed by another. This finding has implications for understanding empathy, learning, and social interactions.

Kübler-Ross Model of Grieving: Elisabeth Kübler-Ross introduced the five stages of grief—denial, anger, bargaining, depression, and acceptance—in her 1969 book "On Death and Dying." These stages have been widely referenced in understanding the process of grieving.

The Hawthorne Effect: This term refers to a type of reactivity in which individuals modify their behavior in response to their awareness of being observed. It originated from a study conducted at the Hawthorne Works of the Western Electric Company.

Martin Seligman's Positive Psychology: Seligman, often called the father of positive psychology, focuses on strengths, well-being, and the pursuit of happiness, contrasting with traditional psychology's focus on dysfunction.

The Flynn Effect: Identified by James R. Flynn, this phenomenon refers to the substantial and long-sustained increase in intelligence test scores measured in many parts of the world over the 20th century.

The Social Identity Theory: Developed by Henri Tajfel and John Turner, this theory examines how group membership and intergroup relationships impact individual self-esteem and behavior.

Economic Theories & Concepts

Adam Smith's Invisible Hand: Smith, often considered the father of modern economics, introduced the concept of the 'invisible hand' in his book "The Wealth of Nations." It describes the unintended social benefits of individual actions when guided by self-interest.

John Maynard Keynes and Keynesian Economics: Keynes

revolutionized economic thinking with his theory that government intervention is necessary to stabilize economies and stimulate demand during economic downturns. His ideas formed the basis of Keynesian economics.

The Nash Equilibrium: Named after mathematician John Nash, the Nash Equilibrium is a concept within game theory where, in a non-cooperative game, no player can benefit by changing their strategy while the other players keep theirs unchanged.

Milton Friedman and Monetarism: Friedman was a leading proponent of monetarism, which emphasizes the role of governments in controlling the amount of money in circulation. He argued that inflation is always and everywhere a monetary phenomenon.

The Laffer Curve: Proposed by economist Arthur Laffer, this curve illustrates a theoretical relationship between rates of taxation and the resulting levels of government revenue. It suggests that there is an optimal tax rate that maximizes revenue without discouraging economic activity.

Karl Marx's Critique of Capitalism: Marx's economic theories, outlined in works like "Das Kapital," provide a critique of capitalism, focusing on its dynamics, internal contradictions, and the inevitable tension between capital and labor.

The Tragedy of the Commons: A concept popularized by Garrett Hardin in 1968, it describes how individuals acting independently according to their self-interest can ultimately destroy a shared resource, even when it's clear that it's not in anyone's long-term interest.

Behavioral Economics: Pioneered by psychologists Daniel Kahneman and Amos Tversky, behavioral economics studies the effects of psychological, cognitive, emotional, cultural, and social factors on economic decisions.

The Concept of Gross Domestic Product (GDP): GDP, a standard measure of a nation's economic performance, was developed by Simon Kuznets in the 1930s. It represents the total value of all goods and services produced over a specific time period within a nation's borders.

Friedrich Hayek and the Austrian School: Hayek, a central figure in the Austrian School of Economics, emphasized the spontaneous order of free markets and the limitations of central planning. His work had a significant influence on libertarian and conservative movements.

The Phillips Curve: Identified by economist A.W. Phillips, the Phillips Curve demonstrates an inverse relationship between unemployment and inflation. It has been a pivotal concept in monetary policy, although its applicability has been debated over time.

Joseph Stiglitz and Information Asymmetry: Nobel laureate Joseph Stiglitz contributed significantly to the understanding of markets with asymmetric information, where one party has more or better information than the other, often leading to market inefficiencies.

Thomas Malthus and Malthusian Theory: Malthus, an English economist and demographer, is famous for his theory that population growth will always tend to outrun the food supply and that betterment of humankind is impossible without strict limits on reproduction.

The Ricardian Model of Comparative Advantage: David Ricardo introduced the theory of comparative advantage, suggesting that even if a country can produce everything more efficiently than another country, it still can benefit from trade.

The Concept of Human Capital: Gary Becker, a pioneer in the field of human capital, explored how investments in education, training, and health can enhance one's productivity and economic value.

Amartya Sen's Capabilities Approach: Nobel Prize-winning economist Amartya Sen developed the capabilities approach, focusing on what individuals are able to do and be, in contrast to traditional focus on income or utility.

The Kuznets Curve: Simon Kuznets, an American economist, hypothesized that as an economy develops, market forces first increase and then decrease economic inequality - illustrated in the shape of an inverted U-curve.

Robert Shiller's Work on Market Volatility: Known for his work on behavioral finance, Shiller has explored how human psychology affects economic decisions and contributes to market volatility, particularly in housing markets and stock prices.

The Gini Coefficient: Developed by Corrado Gini, the Gini coefficient is a measure of income inequality within a population, ranging from 0 (perfect equality) to 1 (perfect inequality).

Elinor Ostrom's Work on Commons Management: Ostrom's research challenged the Tragedy of the Commons, showing how local property can be successfully managed by community organizations rather than centralized institutions.

Cinema & Film Making

The Lumière Brothers and the Birth of Cinema: Auguste and Louis Lumière are credited with the birth of cinema. In 1895, they held the first public movie screening of a series of short scenes from everyday French life.

The First Feature-Length Film: The first feature-length multi-reel film was the Australian production "The Story of the Kelly

Gang" (1906). It ran for more than an hour and pioneered the feature film format.

Alfred Hitchcock's "Psycho" Shower Scene: One of the most iconic scenes in film history, the shower scene in Alfred Hitchcock's "Psycho" (1960), used 77 different camera angles and 50 cuts for a scene that lasted less than three minutes.

The Wizard of Oz's Technicolor: "The Wizard of Oz" (1939) was one of the first films to use Technicolor and is known for its use of vibrant colors, notably the transition from the sepia-toned Kansas to the colorful Land of Oz.

Orson Welles' "Citizen Kane": Often cited as the greatest film ever made, "Citizen Kane" (1941) by Orson Welles revolutionized many aspects of film making with its innovative cinematography, narrative structure, and music.

The Introduction of CGI: "Westworld" (1973) was the first feature film to use digital image processing to pixellate photography to simulate an android's point of view, marking the early beginnings of computer-generated imagery (CGI) in cinema.

The Star Wars Franchise: Created by George Lucas, "Star Wars" (1977) revolutionized special effects and set a new standard for sci-fi movies. Its use of advanced model-making, digital effects, and sound design had a lasting impact on the industry.

The Bollywood Industry: India's film industry, particularly Bollywood, produces the largest number of films annually. Bollywood is known for its colorful, music-filled films that often blend drama, comedy, action, and romance.

The Impact of "Jaws" and the Summer Blockbuster:
Directed by Steven Spielberg, "Jaws" (1975) was the first major summer blockbuster, changing how movies are released and marketed. It established the summer season as a key time for studios to release their biggest hits.

The Rise of Independent Cinema: In the late 20th and early 21st centuries, independent films gained significant attention and acclaim, challenging the dominance of major studios and bringing fresh perspectives and innovative storytelling to the forefront.

The First Talkie: "The Jazz Singer" (1927) was the first feature-length motion picture with synchronized dialogue sequences, heralding the end of the silent film era and the rise of "talkies."

Italian Neorealism: Post-World War II, Italian Neorealism emerged as a significant film movement. Films like Vittorio De Sica's "Bicycle Thieves" (1948) were characterized by stories set amongst the poor and working class, filmed on location, often using non-professional actors.

The French New Wave: A group of French filmmakers, including Jean-Luc Godard and François Truffaut, in the late 1950s and 1960s, revolutionized cinema with their stylistic innovations, narrative techniques, and rejection of traditional filmmaking conventions.

Spielberg's Influence on Modern Cinema: Steven Spielberg is one of the most influential figures in the film industry, known for blockbuster hits and critically acclaimed films spanning diverse genres, from "E.T. the Extra-Terrestrial" to "Schindler's List."

The Advent of Digital Cinematography: The shift from film to digital cinematography marked a significant change in how movies are made. "Collateral" (2004), directed by Michael Mann, was one of the first major films to be shot primarily with high-definition digital cameras.

The Marvel Cinematic Universe: The Marvel Cinematic Universe is a groundbreaking franchise in terms of scale and interconnected storytelling. It has redefined the concept of movie franchises, creating a shared universe across numerous films and series.

Hitchcock's "Vertigo" and Cinematic Innovations: Alfred Hitchcock's "Vertigo" (1958) is notable for its innovative use of the dolly zoom effect, which creates a disorienting vertigo sensation, now commonly known as the "Hitchcock zoom."

The "Lord of the Rings" Trilogy's Technological Advances: Directed by Peter Jackson, these films were notable for their groundbreaking use of computer-generated imagery, including the creation of the character Gollum using motion capture technology.

The Oscars (Academy Awards): Established in 1929, the Oscars are one of the oldest and most prestigious awards in the film industry, recognizing excellence in cinematic achievements.

"Parasite's" Historic Oscar Win: In 2020, Bong Joon-ho's

"Parasite" became the first non-English language film to win the Academy Award for Best Picture, marking a significant moment in the recognition of international cinema.

Great Inventions of the 20th Century

The Invention of the Airplane: The Wright brothers, Orville and Wilbur Wright, achieved the first powered, sustained, and controlled airplane flight on December 17, 1903. This breakthrough laid the foundation for modern aviation.

The Development of Penicillin: Discovered by Alexander Fleming in 1928 and later developed as a medicine by Howard

Florey and Ernst Boris Chain, penicillin was the world's first true antibiotic. It revolutionized the treatment of bacterial infections and saved countless lives.

The Birth of the Internet: The foundation of the internet was laid by the creation of ARPANET in 1969, a project funded by the U.S. Department of Defense. The Internet has since become integral to global communication, commerce, and entertainment.

The Personal Computer Revolution: The launch of the IBM Personal Computer in 1981 is often considered the start of the PC revolution. It made computing accessible to the masses, changing the way people work, learn, and communicate.

The First Mobile Phone: In 1973, Martin Cooper, a Motorola researcher and executive, made the first mobile telephone call using a prototype of what would become the Motorola DynaTAC 8000x, the world's first commercially available handheld cellular phone.

Television Changes Entertainment: Philo Farnsworth invented the first electronic television in 1927, dramatically changing entertainment, news broadcasting, and advertising, and becoming a cornerstone of modern culture and media.

Insulin's Life-Saving Role: In 1922, insulin was first used to treat diabetes. Frederick Banting and Charles Best discovered insulin, transforming diabetes from a fatal diagnosis to a manageable condition.

The Discovery of DNA Structure: In 1953, James Watson and Francis Crick proposed the double helix structure of DNA, paving the way for modern genetics and biotechnology.

The Invention of the Microwave Oven: Percy Spencer accidentally discovered microwave cooking in 1946 when a candy bar in his pocket melted while working on radar equipment. The first commercial microwave oven was released in 1947 by Raytheon.

The Digital Camera and Photography: The first digital camera was developed in 1975 by an engineer at Eastman Kodak named Steve Sasson. It signaled the beginning of a transition from film to digital photography.

The Introduction of Plastic: Although the development of synthetic plastics began in the 19th century, it was in the 20th century that plastics truly transformed manufacturing and product design. Bakelite, invented in 1907 by Leo Baekeland, was the first fully synthetic plastic and marked the beginning of the age of plastics.

The Breakthrough of Nuclear Energy: The first controlled nuclear chain reaction, initiated in 1942 as part of the Manhattan Project, led to the development of nuclear power and nuclear weapons, significantly influencing global politics and energy.

The Contraceptive Pill: Introduced in the 1960s, the birth control pill was a pivotal factor in the sexual revolution, granting women greater control over their reproductive health and contributing to significant societal shifts.

The Invention of the Laser: The first working laser was demonstrated in 1960 by Theodore Maiman. Lasers have since found a vast array of applications, from medicine and communications to entertainment and research.

The ATM Revolutionizes Banking: The first automated teller machine (ATM) was installed in 1967 in London. ATMs revolutionized banking by allowing customers to perform transactions without a teller.

The Invention of Velcro: Velcro was invented in 1948 by Swiss engineer George de Mestral after he noticed how burrs stuck to his dog's fur. It became widely used in various applications, from clothing to aerospace.

GPS Technology: The Global Positioning System (GPS), a satellite-based navigation system, became fully operational in 1995. Originally developed for military use, it is now integral to numerous civilian applications.

The Development of the Heart Pacemaker: The first implantable pacemaker was developed in 1958. This device has since become crucial in treating heart rhythm disorders, significantly improving the quality of life for many patients.

The Invention of Kevlar: In 1965, DuPont chemist Stephanie Kwolek invented Kevlar, a material five times stronger than steel and resistant to wear and corrosion. It's used in products like bulletproof vests and sports equipment.

The Rise of Video Games: The first commercially successful video game, Pong, was released in 1972. Video games have since evolved into a major entertainment industry, influencing culture and social interactions.

Computer Science & The Internet

Alan Turing and the Foundations of Computing: Alan Turing, often considered the father of computer science, laid the groundwork for modern computing with his concept of the Turing machine. He also played a pivotal role in breaking the Enigma code during World War II.

The Creation of the World Wide Web: In 1989, Tim Berners-

Lee, a British computer scientist, invented the World Wide Web while working at CERN. The web fundamentally changed how information is shared and accessed.

The First Computer Virus: The first computer virus, called "Creeper," was created in 1971. It was an experimental self-replicating program written by Bob Thomas at BBN Technologies and was designed to test the security of early networked computing systems.

The Development of Google: Larry Page and Sergey Brin, Ph.D. students at Stanford University, developed Google in 1998. It started as a research project and quickly became the world's most popular search engine, revolutionizing how information is searched and accessed online.

The Invention of the Microprocessor: The microprocessor, a compact unit containing a computer's central processing unit (CPU), was developed in the early 1970s. The Intel 4004, released in 1971, is generally regarded as the first microprocessor.

The Rise of Social Media: The launch of platforms like Facebook (2004), Twitter (2006), and Instagram (2010) has significantly impacted social interaction, media consumption, and even political discourse.

Apple's Innovation with the iPhone: In 2007, Apple released the first iPhone, revolutionizing the mobile phone industry with its touchscreen interface and combination of phone, internet, and media capabilities.

The Significance of Open Source Software: The open-source software movement, championed by figures like Linus Torvalds with the Linux operating system, has been instrumental in the development of the internet and software industry.

Quantum Computing: Quantum computing, which utilizes the principles of quantum mechanics, is an emerging field promising to revolutionize computing by performing complex calculations at unprecedented speeds.

Artificial Intelligence Breakthroughs: The development of AI and machine learning has led to significant advancements in fields like natural language processing, image recognition, and predictive analytics, opening new frontiers in technology and research.

The First Programmable Computer: The Z3, created by German engineer Konrad Zuse in 1941, is considered the first programmable computer. It was used for aerodynamic calculations but was destroyed during World War II.

Email's Early Beginnings: The first email was sent by Ray Tomlinson in 1971. Tomlinson's breakthrough of sending messages between machines via a network laid the groundwork for modern email systems.

The Emergence of E-Commerce: Amazon, founded by Jeff Bezos in 1994, started as an online bookstore and expanded rapidly, playing a key role in the growth of online shopping and the transformation of global retail.

The Concept of the Metaverse: The term "metaverse" was first coined by author Neal Stephenson in his 1992 science fiction novel "Snow Crash." It refers to a collective virtual shared space, created by the convergence of virtually enhanced physical and digital reality.

Blockchain Technology and Cryptocurrency: The launch of Bitcoin in 2009 by an individual or group under the pseudonym Satoshi Nakamoto introduced the concept of blockchain, a decentralized ledger system, which has significant implications beyond cryptocurrencies.

Wi-Fi's Development: The foundational technology for Wi-Fi was developed in the 1990s by a team led by Dr. John O'Sullivan in Australia. It has become a crucial technology for wireless networking globally.

The Development of GPS: The Global Positioning System (GPS), originally developed by the U.S. Department of Defense for military navigation, became widely available for civilian use in the 1980s and has since become integral to navigation and mapping services.

The Invention of the Mouse: The computer mouse, a pivotal device for graphical interfaces, was invented by Douglas Engelbart in 1963. Its development was part of a larger project to augment human intellect.

Voice Recognition Technology: Significant advances in voice recognition technology have led to the development of virtual assistants like Apple's Siri, Amazon's Alexa, and Google Assistant, changing the way users interact with their devices.

The Growth of Streaming Services: The rise of streaming platforms like Netflix, which started as a DVD rental service, has revolutionized the media and entertainment industries, leading to a shift from traditional cable TV to on-demand streaming.

Famous Explorers & Expeditions

Christopher Columbus' Voyage to the New World: In 1492, Christopher Columbus embarked on his first voyage across the Atlantic Ocean, aiming to find a westward route to Asia. Instead, he landed in the New World, opening up the Americas to European exploration.

Marco Polo's Travels to Asia: Venetian merchant Marco Polo traveled to Asia along the Silk Road between 1271 and 1295. His detailed accounts of his experiences in the book "The Travels of Marco Polo" provided Europeans with a rare insight into Asian lands and cultures.

Ernest Shackleton's Antarctic Expedition: Shackleton's 1914-1917 Imperial Trans-Antarctic Expedition aboard the ship Endurance is renowned for its story of survival. After Endurance was trapped and crushed by ice, Shackleton and his crew endured a harrowing journey to safety.

Ferdinand Magellan's Circumnavigation: Magellan embarked on the first expedition to circumnavigate the globe in 1519. Although Magellan was killed in the Philippines, his fleet completed the journey, proving that the Earth is round and much larger than previously thought.

Lewis and Clark's Expedition: Commissioned by President Thomas Jefferson, Meriwether Lewis and William Clark led an expedition from 1804 to 1806 across the western United States. Their journey provided valuable information about the geography, flora, fauna, and native cultures of the American West.

Amelia Earhart's Aviation Pioneering: Earhart was a pioneering aviator and the first female pilot to fly solo across the Atlantic Ocean. Her disappearance in 1937 during an attempt to circumnavigate the globe remains one of the greatest unsolved mysteries.

Vasco da Gama's Route to India: In 1498, Portuguese explorer Vasco da Gama became the first European to reach India by sea, opening up a direct trade route with Asia and heralding a new era in global commerce.

Roald Amundsen's Race to the South Pole: Norwegian explorer Roald Amundsen was the first to reach the South Pole in 1911, beating British explorer Robert Falcon Scott in a historic race.

Zheng He's Treasure Fleet: Chinese admiral Zheng He led seven naval expeditions in the early 15th century, traveling to Southeast Asia, India, the Middle East, and Africa, and showcasing the power and reach of the Ming Dynasty.

The Apollo Moon Landings: The United States' Apollo space program, particularly Apollo 11 in 1969, marked the first time humans walked on the moon, a milestone in space exploration and human achievement.

David Livingstone's African Expeditions: Scottish explorer David Livingstone is famous for his extensive explorations in Africa, aiming to find the source of the Nile River. His encounters, including being found by Henry Morton Stanley with the famous phrase "Dr. Livingstone, I presume?" have become legendary.

Neil Armstrong and the First Moonwalk: As the commander of NASA's Apollo 11 mission, Neil Armstrong became the first person to walk on the moon in 1969, marking a monumental milestone in human space exploration.

Jacques Cousteau's Underwater Exploration: French naval officer and explorer Jacques Cousteau co-invented the Aqua-Lung, an early version of scuba gear, and conducted extensive underwater expeditions, significantly contributing to oceanography.

Hernán Cortés and the Aztec Empire: Spanish Conquistador Hernán Cortés is known for his 1519 expedition that led to the fall of the Aztec Empire. His encounters with the Aztecs and the eventual conquest of Mexico are crucial in the history of Spanish colonization.

The Journeys of Ibn Battuta: Ibn Battuta, a Moroccan explorer, traveled more extensively than any other explorer in pre-modern history, covering much of the Islamic world as well as many non-Muslim lands from 1325 to 1354.

James Cook's Voyages to the Pacific: British explorer James Cook made three voyages to the Pacific Ocean, achieving the first recorded European contact with the eastern coastline of Australia and the Hawaiian Islands, and the first circumnavigation of New Zealand.

Matthew Henson's Arctic Achievements: American explorer Matthew Henson, alongside Robert Peary, is best known for their expeditions to the North Pole. Henson, an African American, is often credited as the first person to reach the geographic North Pole.

Yuri Gagarin's Historic Spaceflight: Soviet cosmonaut Yuri Gagarin became the first human to journey into outer space and orbit the Earth in 1961, a significant achievement in the space race.

Juan Ponce de León and the Search for the Fountain of Youth: Spanish explorer Juan Ponce de León is known for his 1513 expedition to Florida, which he initially approached in search of the mythical Fountain of Youth.

Gertrude Bell's Middle Eastern Expeditions: English writer, traveler, and political officer Gertrude Bell played a significant role in British imperial policy-making in the Middle East, particularly in Iraq, during and after World War I.

Volcanoes & Earthquakes

The Eruption of Mount Vesuvius: In 79 AD, the eruption of Mount Vesuvius in Italy buried the cities of Pompeii and Herculaneum under ash and pumice. The event, frozen in time, provides valuable historical insight into Roman life.

The 2011 Tohoku Earthquake and Tsunami: This magnitude 9.0–9.1 undersea earthquake off the coast of Japan triggered powerful tsunami waves that caused widespread destruction and the Fukushima Daiichi nuclear disaster, one of the most significant nuclear accidents in history.

The Ring of Fire: The Pacific Ring of Fire is an area with a high level of tectonic activity, including a large number of earthquakes and volcanic eruptions. It's home to 75% of the world's active and dormant volcanoes.

Krakatoa's 1883 Eruption: The 1883 eruption of Krakatoa in Indonesia is one of the deadliest and most destructive volcanic events in recorded history, with the explosions heard as far away as Australia.

Yellowstone Supervolcano: The Yellowstone Caldera, a supervolcano located in Yellowstone National Park, has had three massive eruptions, with the most recent occurring approximately 640,000 years ago. Its potential future activity is closely monitored.

The San Andreas Fault: Running through California, the San Andreas Fault is a continental transform fault that forms the tectonic boundary between the Pacific Plate and the North American Plate, and is famous for producing significant and devastating earthquakes.

Mount St. Helens' 1980 Eruption: This eruption in Washington, USA, was the deadliest and most economically destructive volcanic event in U.S. history, causing 57 deaths and massive destruction of property.

The Concept of Seismic Waves: Seismic waves, generated by earthquakes, are used by geologists to study the Earth's interior. There are different types of seismic waves, including P-waves, S-waves, and surface waves.

The Great Lisbon Earthquake of 1755: This devastating earthquake, followed by a tsunami and fires, struck Portugal and significantly influenced philosophical and scientific thought in Europe, leading to the development of modern seismology.

Pliny the Younger's Account of Vesuvius: Pliny the Younger, a Roman writer and administrator, provided one of the earliest eyewitness accounts of a volcanic eruption, describing the eruption of Mount Vesuvius in letters to the historian Tacitus.

The 2004 Indian Ocean Earthquake and Tsunami: One of the deadliest natural disasters in recorded history, this undersea megathrust earthquake off the coast of Sumatra, Indonesia, triggered a series of devastating tsunamis, affecting several countries and resulting in over 230,000 deaths.

The Formation of the Hawaiian Islands: The Hawaiian Islands were formed by volcanic activity initiated at an undersea magma source called the Hawaii hotspot. Kilauea and Mauna Loa, two of the world's most active volcanoes, are located in Hawaii.

The Tangshan Earthquake of 1976: One of the largest earthquakes of the 20th century, this earthquake in China is believed to have killed between 240,000 to 655,000 people, making it one of the deadliest in history.

Mount Tambora's 1815 Eruption: The eruption of Mount Tambora in Indonesia in 1815 is the most powerful volcanic eruption in recorded history. It led to the "Year Without a Summer" in 1816 due to the massive amounts of volcanic ash propelled into the upper atmosphere.

The Loma Prieta Earthquake of 1989: This earthquake, occurring in the San Francisco Bay Area, was notable for its live broadcast during the 1989 World Series. It caused significant damage and loss of life and led to changes in earthquake preparedness and response strategies.

The Discovery of Pompeii: The city of Pompeii, buried by the eruption of Mount Vesuvius in 79 AD, was rediscovered in 1748. Excavations have provided an extraordinarily detailed insight into the life of a city during the Pax Romana.

Volcanic Ash's Effect on Aviation: The 2010 eruption of Eyjafjallajökull in Iceland caused enormous disruption to air travel across western and northern Europe over six days. It highlighted the significant impact of volcanic ash on aviation safety.

The Great Chilean Earthquake of 1960: The most powerful earthquake ever recorded, this magnitude 9.5 earthquake occurred in Chile. It caused widespread damage in Chile and generated tsunamis that affected distant locations like Hawaii, Japan, and the Philippines.

Vesuvius' Ongoing Threat: Mount Vesuvius remains one of the world's most dangerous volcanoes due to its history of explosive eruptions and the dense population living nearby in the city of Naples.

The Importance of Earthquake-Resistant Construction:
Following major earthquakes in urban areas, there has been an increased focus on designing earthquake-resistant structures, especially in regions with high seismic activity.

Renewable Energy and Resources

The Rise of Solar Power: The photovoltaic effect, the basis for solar panels, was discovered by French physicist Edmond Becquerel in 1839. Today, solar power is one of the fastest-growing renewable energy sources worldwide.

Wind Power History: Windmills have been used since the 9th century in the Middle East. Modern wind turbines, generating electricity, began appearing in the late 19th and early 20th centuries, with significant advancements in efficiency and design over the past few decades.

Hydropower's Ancient Roots: Hydropower, using water to generate energy, dates back to Ancient Greece. The modern hydropower industry began with the construction of the first hydroelectric power plant at Niagara Falls in 1879.

Geothermal Energy: The first geothermal power plant was built in 1904 in Larderello, Italy. Geothermal energy harnesses heat from the Earth and is a powerful, sustainable energy source in regions with high volcanic activity.

The Development of Biofuels: Biofuels, such as ethanol and biodiesel, have been around since the invention of the diesel engine. Rudolf Diesel originally designed his engine to run on peanut oil.

The Largest Solar Power Plant: As of my last update, the Bhadla Solar Park in India is one of the largest solar parks in the world, spanning over 10,000 acres and with a capacity of nearly 2,245 MW.

China's Leadership in Renewable Energy: China is a global leader in renewable energy, particularly in solar and wind energy production. It's also the largest producer of hydroelectric power.

The Potential of Tidal Energy: The Rance Tidal Power Station in France, operational since 1966, was the world's first large-scale tidal power plant, harnessing energy from tidal flow.

Advancements in Battery Technology: The development of

efficient, high-capacity batteries is crucial for storing energy from intermittent sources like solar and wind. Lithium-ion batteries are at the forefront of this technology.

Green Hydrogen as a Fuel Source: Green hydrogen, produced by electrolyzing water using renewable energy, is emerging as a potential clean fuel source for industries and transportation, offering a solution for decarbonizing sectors that are difficult to electrify.

The Growth of Offshore Wind Farms: Offshore wind farms take advantage of the stronger and more consistent winds at sea. The world's largest offshore wind farm, Hornsea Project One in the United Kingdom, has a capacity of 1.2 gigawatts.

Solar Roads: Innovations like solar roadways are being explored, where roads are paved with solar panels to generate electricity. The world's first solar road opened in 2014 in the Netherlands.

Wave Energy: This form of renewable energy harnesses the energy of ocean surface waves to generate electricity. The first commercial wave farm was the Aguçadoura Wave Park in Portugal, opened in 2008.

The International Space Station's Use of Solar Energy: The ISS is powered by solar energy, using large solar arrays to convert sunlight into electricity. It's a prime example of solar power's potential in challenging environments.

Tesla's Gigafactory: Tesla's Gigafactory in Nevada, one of the largest battery factories in the world, aims to significantly lower the cost of batteries and make electric vehicles and energy storage more accessible.

Denmark's Wind Power Achievement: In 2019, Denmark generated 47% of its electricity from wind power, the highest percentage from wind by any country, showcasing the potential of wind energy as a major power source.

Net-zero Energy Buildings: These buildings produce as much renewable energy as they consume over the course of a year, making them highly sustainable. The Bullitt Center in Seattle is an example of a commercial building designed to be net-zero.

The Sahara Solar Breeder Project: This ambitious project aims to turn the Sahara Desert into a vast solar farm, capable of providing clean energy to the whole world due to the desert's optimal sunlight conditions.

The Global Rise of Electric Vehicles (EVs): EVs are an important component of reducing greenhouse gas emissions. The Tesla Model 3 became the world's all-time best-selling electric car by early 2020.

Concentrated Solar Power (CSP) Systems: CSP plants, like the Ivanpah Solar Power Facility in the Mojave Desert, use mirrors to concentrate sunlight to drive traditional steam turbines or engines that create electricity.

Influential Women Throughout History

Marie Curie's Groundbreaking Discoveries: Marie Curie was the first woman to win a Nobel Prize and the only person to win in two different scientific fields—Physics and Chemistry. She discovered polonium and radium and conducted pioneering research in radioactivity.

Amelia Earhart's Aviation Pioneering: Amelia Earhart was an aviation pioneer and the first female aviator to fly solo across the Atlantic Ocean. Her efforts in promoting women in aviation were groundbreaking, even though her disappearance during a circumnavigational flight remains a mystery.

Rosa Parks and the Civil Rights Movement: Rosa Parks' refusal to give up her seat on a Montgomery, Alabama bus in 1955 became a pivotal symbol of the Civil Rights Movement, inspiring the Montgomery Bus Boycott.

Malala Yousafzai's Advocacy for Education: Pakistani activist Malala Yousafzai, the youngest-ever Nobel Prize laureate, is known for her advocacy for girls' education in her native Swat Valley and globally, despite an assassination attempt by the Taliban.

Cleopatra's Reign: Cleopatra VII, the last active ruler of the Ptolemaic Kingdom of Egypt, was known for her intelligence, political astuteness, and romantic liaisons with Roman leaders Julius Caesar and Mark Antony.

Ada Lovelace's Contributions to Computing: Ada Lovelace, an English mathematician and writer, worked on Charles Babbage's proposed mechanical general-purpose computer, the Analytical Engine. She is regarded as the first to recognize the full potential of computers and one of the first computer programmers.

Mother Teresa's Humanitarian Work: Mother Teresa, a Roman Catholic nun and missionary, was known for her humanitarian work in helping the poor and sick through the Missionaries of Charity in Kolkata, India. She was canonized as a saint and was awarded the Nobel Peace Prize.

Harriet Tubman and the Underground Railroad: An escaped slave herself, Harriet Tubman was a key figure in the Underground Railroad, a network of secret routes and safe houses used to help enslaved African Americans escape to freedom.

Frida Kahlo's Artistic Expression: Mexican artist Frida Kahlo is celebrated for her deeply personal and vividly colored works, often exploring themes of identity, the human body, and suffering.

Katherine Johnson's Contributions to Space Exploration: Katherine Johnson, an African American mathematician at NASA, played a crucial role in the success of the United States' spaceflights, including the Apollo 11 mission to the moon.

Susan B. Anthony's Fight for Women's Rights: A key figure in the women's suffrage movement in the United States, Susan B. Anthony played a pivotal role in the fight for women's right to vote, leading to the 19th Amendment to the U.S. Constitution.

Marie Stopes' Contributions to Birth Control: British scientist Marie Stopes was a leading advocate for birth control and opened the first birth control clinic in Britain. Her work significantly advanced women's reproductive rights.

Margaret Thatcher's Political Impact: Margaret Thatcher, the first female Prime Minister of the United Kingdom, was one of the most influential political figures of the 20th century, known for her conservative policies and strong leadership style.

Simone de Beauvoir's Influence on Feminist Philosophy: A French writer and philosopher, Simone de Beauvoir's book "The Second Sex" is a foundational tract of contemporary feminism, discussing the treatment of women throughout history.

Hedy Lamarr's Dual Career as Actress and Inventor: Known for her Hollywood career, Hedy Lamarr also co-invented a frequency-hopping technology that later became the basis for Wi-Fi and Bluetooth communication systems.

Wangari Maathai's Environmental Activism: Kenyan environmentalist Wangari Maathai founded the Green Belt Movement, focused on tree planting, conservation, and women's rights. She was the first African woman to receive the Nobel Peace Prize.

Sappho's Contributions to Literature: An ancient Greek poet, Sappho is known for her lyric poetry, written to be sung and accompanied by a lyre. She is one of the first known female writers in Western history.

Valentina Tereshkova's Space Journey: In 1963, Soviet cosmonaut Valentina Tereshkova became the first woman to travel to space. Her solo mission aboard Vostok 6 made her an international icon of female achievement in a male-dominated field.

Indira Gandhi's Leadership: As the first and, to date, only female Prime Minister of India, Indira Gandhi was a central figure in Indian politics, known for her political ruthlessness and unprecedented centralization of power.

Grace Hopper's Pioneering Work in Computing: American computer scientist Grace Hopper was one of the first programmers of the Harvard Mark I computer and developed the first compiler for a computer programming language, laying the foundations for modern software development.

Space Missions and Satellites

The Apollo 11 Moon Landing: On July 20, 1969, Apollo 11 mission astronauts Neil Armstrong and Buzz Aldrin became the first humans to walk on the moon, marking a monumental milestone in space exploration.

The Hubble Space Telescope: Launched in 1990, the Hubble Space Telescope has provided some of the most detailed and distant images of outer space, vastly improving our understanding of the universe.

The Voyager Missions: Voyager 1 and Voyager 2, launched in 1977, have traveled further in space than any other human-made objects. Voyager 1 entered interstellar space in 2012, sending back invaluable data about areas of space previously unexplored by humans.

The International Space Station (ISS): A multinational collaborative project, the ISS serves as a microgravity and space environment research laboratory in which scientific research is conducted in astrobiology, astronomy, meteorology, physics, and other fields.

Sputnik 1 – The First Artificial Satellite: Launched by the Soviet Union in 1957, Sputnik 1 was the world's first artificial satellite, marking the start of the space age and the U.S.-USSR space race.

Mars Rovers Exploration: NASA's Mars rovers, including Spirit, Opportunity, and Curiosity, have been exploring Mars' surface since 2004, providing invaluable information about the Red Planet's geography, climate, and potential for life.

Saturn's Exploration by Cassini-Huygens: The Cassini-Huygens mission, a collaboration between NASA, the European Space Agency, and the Italian Space Agency, spent 13 years exploring Saturn and its moons, making significant discoveries about the planet's rings and natural satellites.

First Woman in Space: In 1963, Soviet cosmonaut Valentina Tereshkova became the first woman to fly in space, orbiting the Earth 48 times in her spacecraft Vostok 6.

The Kepler Space Telescope and Exoplanet Discoveries: NASA's Kepler space telescope, launched in 2009, was dedicated to finding Earth-size planets orbiting other stars. It has discovered thousands of exoplanets, expanding our knowledge of potential life-sustaining planets.

China's Tiangong Space Station: China is actively expanding its presence in space, exemplified by the launch and development of the Tiangong Space Station, marking a significant step in its independent space exploration capabilities.

The New Horizons Pluto Mission: Launched in 2006, NASA's New Horizons spacecraft performed a historic flyby of Pluto in 2015, providing the first close-up images and extensive scientific information about the dwarf planet and its moons.

The First Spacewalk: In 1965, Soviet cosmonaut Alexei Leonov performed the first human spacewalk, exiting his Voskhod 2 spacecraft for 12 minutes and 9 seconds, a pivotal moment in the history of space exploration.

The Galileo Mission to Jupiter: NASA's Galileo spacecraft, launched in 1989, spent eight years orbiting Jupiter, providing detailed data about the gas giant and its moons, particularly Io, Europa, Ganymede, and Callisto.

The Chandra X-ray Observatory: Part of NASA's Great Observatories program, the Chandra X-ray Observatory, launched in 1999, observes X-rays from high-energy regions of the universe, such as the remnants of exploded stars.

SpaceX and Commercial Space Travel: Founded by Elon Musk, SpaceX has been instrumental in advancing commercial space travel. It achieved the first privately-funded spacecraft (Dragon) to reach the International Space Station in 2012.

The Juno Mission to Jupiter: Launched in 2011, NASA's Juno spacecraft entered Jupiter's orbit in 2016 to study the planet's composition, gravity field, magnetic field, and polar magnetosphere.

The Rosetta Comet Mission: The European Space Agency's Rosetta mission, launched in 2004, achieved the first successful landing on a comet nucleus (Comet 67P) in 2014, providing valuable data about comets' composition and structure.

The Discovery of Water on Mars: Mars missions, including those by NASA's Mars Reconnaissance Orbiter and Mars Exploration Rovers, have provided evidence of water in liquid form on Mars, a critical discovery for understanding the planet's potential to support life.

The Parker Solar Probe: Launched in 2018, NASA's Parker Solar Probe is designed to get closer to the Sun than any previous spacecraft, with a mission to study the outer corona of the Sun, solar wind, and space weather.

The Artemis Program: NASA's Artemis program aims to land "the first woman and the next man" on the Moon by 2024, focusing on the lunar south pole region, with plans to establish a sustainable human presence on the Moon by 2028.

Weather Phenomena & Climate

The Formation of Tornadoes: Tornadoes, often associated with supercell thunderstorms, form when warm, moist air collides with cool, dry air, creating a rotating updraft. The U.S. experiences more tornadoes than any other country, particularly in the region known as "Tornado Alley."

The Concept of El Niño: El Niño is a climate pattern that occurs in the Pacific Ocean, causing significant changes in weather patterns globally. It involves the warming of the ocean surface waters in the central and eastern Pacific, leading to dramatic weather changes.

The Discovery of the Jet Stream: The jet stream, a fast flowing river of air high in the atmosphere, was first discovered by Japanese meteorologist Wasaburo Oishi in the 1920s using weather balloons. Jet streams significantly impact weather patterns and aviation routes.

The Power of Hurricanes: Hurricanes, known as typhoons in the Pacific and cyclones in the Indian Ocean, are massive storm systems with wind speeds exceeding 74 mph. The Saffir-Simpson Hurricane Wind Scale is used to classify their intensity.

Aurora Borealis and Aurora Australis: These natural light displays in the Earth's sky, predominantly seen in high-latitude regions around the Arctic and Antarctic, are caused by disturbances in the magnetosphere due to solar wind.

The Intensity of Heatwaves: Heatwaves are prolonged periods of excessively hot weather, which can be more dangerous than other weather phenomena due to their subtle nature. The 2003 European heatwave is considered one of the deadliest, causing thousands of deaths.

The Impact of Climate Change on Weather Patterns: Climate change, largely driven by human activities, is leading to more extreme and unpredictable weather events, including more intense storms, droughts, heatwaves, and changing precipitation patterns.

The Role of Clouds in Weather Prediction: Cloud formation and the types of clouds present can tell meteorologists a lot about impending weather. Luke Howard, a British manufacturing chemist, was the first to introduce a nomenclature system for clouds in 1802.

The Phenomenon of Monsoons: Monsoons are seasonal wind patterns that cause wet and dry seasons throughout much of the tropics. They are critical for agriculture in many regions, particularly in South Asia.

The Creation of Snowflakes: Each snowflake is unique and forms when water vapor in the atmosphere freezes onto a dust particle, creating an ice crystal. The shape of a snowflake is influenced by the temperature and humidity it encounters as it falls to the ground.

The Dust Bowl of the 1930s: This severe drought, combined with decades of agricultural mismanagement, led to wind erosion that turned the American and Canadian prairies into dust bowls. This period prompted significant changes in farming practices and environmental policy.

Lightning and Its Power: A single lightning bolt can heat the air around it to temperatures five times hotter than the sun's surface. The phenomenon of "ball lightning" remains one of the more mysterious weather events, with scientists still trying to fully understand its nature.

The Record for the Highest Temperature: The highest air temperature ever recorded on Earth was 134.1°F (56.7°C) in Furnace Creek Ranch, Death Valley, California, in 1913. However, this record is subject to debate and scrutiny among meteorologists.

The Concept of Microclimates: Microclimates are areas with climate conditions that differ from the surrounding areas. They can be naturally occurring or influenced by human activities, and they demonstrate how local landscapes and urban environments can impact weather patterns.

The Great Galveston Hurricane of 1900: The deadliest natural disaster in U.S. history, this hurricane struck Galveston, Texas, and resulted in an estimated 6,000 to 12,000 fatalities. The disaster led to major improvements in hurricane forecasting and preparedness.

The Phenomenon of La Niña: La Niña, the counterpart to El Niño, is characterized by unusually cold ocean temperatures in the Equatorial Pacific. It has widespread effects on weather around the world, often including increased rainfall in some areas and drought in others.

The Greenland Ice Sheet and Climate: The Greenland Ice Sheet, the second-largest ice body in the world, is a critical indicator of climate change. Its melting contributes to global sea level rise and influences ocean circulation patterns.

The Discovery of the Ozone Hole: In the 1980s, scientists discovered a hole in the ozone layer over Antarctica, leading to global efforts to phase out ozone-depleting substances like chlorofluorocarbons (CFCs).

The Indian Ocean Dipole: Similar to El Niño in the Pacific, the Indian Ocean Dipole affects climate patterns in the Indian Ocean region. It involves phases of warmer and cooler sea surface temperatures, influencing weather events like monsoons and droughts.

The 2005 Atlantic Hurricane Season: This season was the most active Atlantic hurricane season recorded, with 28 named storms, including Hurricane Katrina. It prompted extensive discussion about the impact of global warming on the frequency and intensity of hurricanes.

Philosophy & Great Thinkers

Socrates' Method of Inquiry: Socrates, an ancient Greek philosopher, is renowned for his contribution to the field of ethics and his method of inquiry, known as the Socratic method, which involved asking probing questions to stimulate critical thinking.

Plato's Academy: Plato, a student of Socrates, founded the

Academy in Athens around 387 BC. It is considered the first institution of higher learning in the Western world, where he taught philosophy and inspired future philosophers, including his most famous student, Aristotle.

Aristotle's Wide-Ranging Influence: Aristotle's works covered a vast array of subjects, including physics, biology, metaphysics, logic, ethics, aesthetics, poetry, theater, music, rhetoric, psychology, linguistics, economics, and politics. His ideas profoundly influenced Western intellectual history.

Confucius and Eastern Philosophy: Confucius, an ancient Chinese philosopher, founded a school of thought known as Confucianism, which emphasizes personal and governmental morality, correctness of social relationships, justice, and sincerity.

Immanuel Kant and Modern Philosophy: Kant is a central figure in modern philosophy, who synthesized early modern rationalism and empiricism, set the terms for much of nineteenth and twentieth-century philosophy, and continues to exercise a significant influence today.

The Existentialism of Jean-Paul Sartre and Simone de Beauvoir: Jean-Paul Sartre and Simone de Beauvoir were key figures in the existentialist movement, exploring themes of freedom, responsibility, and the meaning of life in their philosophical and literary works.

Friedrich Nietzsche's Philosophy: Nietzsche's work has exerted a profound influence on modern intellectual history. He challenged the foundations of Christianity and traditional morality, famous for his statement "God is dead."

The Social Contract Theory of John Locke: Locke's theories of the social contract, as well as his views on natural rights, property, and the separation of powers, were foundational in the development of modern liberal democracy.

Eastern Philosophy's Influence: Alongside Confucianism, other Eastern philosophical traditions like Taoism and Buddhism have contributed significantly to the global philosophical landscape, offering perspectives on harmony, balance, and the nature of suffering.

The Pragmatism of William James and John Dewey: Pragmatism, an American philosophical tradition started by C.S. Peirce and developed by William James and John Dewey, emphasizes the practical application of ideas by acting on them to actually test them in human experiences.

René Descartes' Cogito: René Descartes, a French philosopher, mathematician, and scientist, is famous for his statement "Cogito, ergo sum" (I think, therefore I am). His work laid the groundwork for 17th-century Continental rationalism, later called Cartesianism.

The Stoicism of Marcus Aurelius: Marcus Aurelius, a Roman Emperor and philosopher, is best known for his work "Meditations," which offers guidance on how to apply Stoic philosophy in daily life, emphasizing duty, self-discipline, and rationality.

Ludwig Wittgenstein's Language Philosophy: Wittgenstein was an Austrian-British philosopher who worked primarily in logic, the philosophy of mathematics, the philosophy of mind, and the philosophy of language, famously stating, "The limits of my language mean the limits of my world."

Karl Marx's Political and Economic Theories: Marx, a philosopher, economist, historian, sociologist, political theorist, journalist, and socialist revolutionary, is best known for his theories about capitalism and communism, co-authoring "The Communist Manifesto."

Thomas Aquinas' Integration of Aristotle with Christian Doctrine: Aquinas was an Italian Dominican friar and Catholic priest who was an immensely influential philosopher and theologian in the tradition of scholasticism, known for synthesizing Aristotelian philosophy with Christian doctrine.

David Hume's Empiricism: A Scottish Enlightenment philosopher, Hume is known for his skepticism and empiricism, challenging traditional notions of causality and personal identity.

Bertrand Russell's Analytic Philosophy: Russell was a British philosopher, logician, mathematician, historian, writer, social critic, and political activist, known for his work in analytic philosophy and for his influence on modern logic and philosophical empiricism.

Simone Weil's Philosophical and Spiritual Quest: Weil, a French philosopher and political activist, combined social and political philosophy with mysticism, exploring themes of suffering, beauty, and the nature of good and evil.

The African Philosophy of Ubuntu: Ubuntu is a Nguni Bantu term meaning "humanity." It is often translated as "I am because we are," and is a philosophy from Southern Africa that emphasizes community, sharing, and generosity.

Hannah Arendt's Exploration of Totalitarianism: Arendt, a German-American philosopher and political theorist, is known for her works on the nature of power and evil, as well as democracy and totalitarianism, particularly in her book "The Origins of Totalitarianism."

Political Systems & Movements

The Origin of Democracy in Ancient Greece: Democracy, as a system of government, began in ancient Athens around 507 BC under the leadership of Cleisthenes. It was a direct form of democracy, where citizens voted on legislation and executive bills in their own right.

The Rise of Communism with Karl Marx: The ideology of

communism, as laid out by Karl Marx and Friedrich Engels in "The Communist Manifesto," advocated for a classless society in which all property is publicly owned, and each person works and is paid according to their abilities and needs.

The American Revolution and the Birth of Modern Democracy: The American Revolution (1765–1783) led to the creation of the United States, a democratic republic, with its Constitution becoming a landmark document of modern democracy.

The French Revolution and the Rise of Republics: The French Revolution (1789–1799) was a period of radical social and political upheaval in France that had a lasting impact on French and world history, leading to the rise of the French Republic.

The Impact of Capitalism and Adam Smith: Capitalism as an economic system gained prominence with the publication of Adam Smith's "The Wealth of Nations" in 1776, advocating for free markets, competition, and the 'invisible hand' of supply and demand.

The Women's Suffrage Movement: The fight for women's voting rights was a significant political movement across the globe, with New Zealand becoming the first country to grant women the right to vote in 1893.

The Bolshevik Revolution: The 1917 Russian Revolution led by Vladimir Lenin and the Bolsheviks was a pivotal event that led to the formation of the Soviet Union, the world's first communist state.

The Civil Rights Movement in the United States: This movement, particularly prominent during the 1950s and 1960s, fought to end racial segregation and discrimination against African Americans, led by figures like Martin Luther King Jr. and Rosa Parks.

The Fall of the Berlin Wall and the End of the Cold War: The fall of the Berlin Wall in 1989 symbolized the end of the Cold War and was a key moment in the collapse of communism in Eastern Europe.

The Arab Spring: Beginning in 2010, this series of anti-government protests, uprisings, and armed rebellions spread across much of the Arab world, marking a significant period of political and social turmoil in the region.

The Non-Aligned Movement: Originating during the Cold War, the Non-Aligned Movement was formed by countries that sought to remain independent from the influence of the major power blocs (the United States and the Soviet Union). It played a significant role in international relations during the 20th century.

The Magna Carta and Constitutional Monarchy: Signed in 1215, the Magna Carta was a charter agreed upon by King John of England that promised the protection of church rights, protection from illegal imprisonment, access to swift justice, and limitations on feudal payments to the Crown.

Fascism in Italy and Nazism in Germany: Fascism, led by Benito Mussolini in Italy, and Nazism, under Adolf Hitler in Germany, were authoritarian political movements that rose to power in the early 20th century, leading to World War II and the Holocaust.

Mao Zedong and the Chinese Communist Revolution: Mao Zedong led the Chinese Communist Revolution, culminating in the establishment of the People's Republic of China in 1949, significantly altering the political and social landscape of China.

The Welfare State Concept: The concept of the welfare state, where the government plays a key role in the protection and promotion of the economic and social well-being of its citizens, gained prominence after World War II, especially in Europe.

The Green Movement and Environmental Politics: Beginning in the 1970s, the Green Movement has grown worldwide, emphasizing environmental issues, sustainable development, and conservation efforts, influencing political policies globally.

The Velvet Revolution and the Collapse of Communism in Czechoslovakia: The Velvet Revolution in 1989 was a non-violent transition of power in what was then Czechoslovakia, marking the end of Communist rule in the country.

The Rise of Populism in the 21st Century: The early 21st century has seen a rise in populist movements and leaders, characterized by anti-establishment sentiments, opposition to globalization, and often nationalistic tendencies.

The Iranian Revolution of 1979: The Iranian Revolution resulted in the overthrow of the Pahlavi dynasty and the establishment of an Islamic Republic under Ayatollah Khomeini, dramatically changing the geopolitical landscape of the Middle East.

The Decolonization Movement Post World War II: Following World War II, a wave of decolonization swept across Asia and Africa, leading to the independence of several nations from colonial powers and a significant reshaping of international relations.

Underwater Exploration

Jacques Cousteau's Contributions: Jacques Cousteau, a French naval officer, explorer, and conservationist, co-developed the Aqua-Lung, an early model of the scuba gear, greatly enhancing the ability to explore underwater.

The Discovery of the Titanic Wreckage: The wreckage of the RMS Titanic, which sank in 1912, was discovered in 1985 by a team led by Robert Ballard. It lies at a depth of about 12,500 feet (3,800 meters) in the North Atlantic Ocean.

The First Untethered Submersible Dive: In 1960, the bathyscaphe Trieste, piloted by Jacques Piccard and Don Walsh, made the first successful dive to the Challenger Deep, the deepest known point in the ocean.

Coral Reef Ecosystems: Coral reefs, often referred to as "rainforests of the sea," are some of the most diverse and valuable ecosystems on Earth. They provide habitat for millions of marine species.

The Great Barrier Reef: The Great Barrier Reef off the coast of Australia is the world's largest coral reef system and can be seen from space. It spans over 1,400 miles (2,300 kilometers) and is a hotspot for biodiversity.

Hydrothermal Vents and Deep-Sea Life: Discovered in the late 1970s, hydrothermal vents are openings in the seafloor that emit hot, mineral-rich water, supporting unique ecosystems with organisms adapted to extreme conditions.

The Evolution of Diving Technology: From early diving bells to modern advanced scuba gear and submersibles like Alvin, the evolution of diving technology has dramatically expanded our ability to explore and study the ocean depths.

Underwater Archaeology: Sunken ships, submerged cities, and ancient artifacts discovered through underwater archaeology provide invaluable insights into human history and maritime heritage.

The Blue Hole Explorations: Blue holes, large marine

sinkholes, have been explored by divers like Jacques Cousteau and more recently by teams using advanced technology, revealing secrets about marine life, geology, and climate change.The Deep Sea Challenger Expedition: In 2012, filmmaker James Cameron piloted the Deepsea Challenger to the bottom of the Mariana Trench, reaching a depth of 35,787 feet (10,908 meters), and becoming the first person to do so solo.

The Sinking of the Lusitania: The wreck of the RMS Lusitania, a British ocean liner sunk by a German U-boat in 1915, was discovered in 1935. Its sinking was a significant event in World War I, contributing to the United States' decision to enter the war.

The Discovery of the Antikythera Mechanism: Discovered in a shipwreck off the Greek island of Antikythera in 1901, the Antikythera Mechanism is an ancient Greek analog computer used to predict astronomical positions and eclipses for calendrical and astrological purposes.

The Underwater Exploration of Lake Baikal: Russia's Lake Baikal, the deepest and oldest freshwater lake in the world, has been the site of numerous scientific explorations, revealing unique species and offering insights into freshwater ecology.

Artificial Reefs and Marine Conservation: Sunk ships and other structures have been used to create artificial reefs, encouraging marine life growth and aiding in ocean conservation efforts.

The Silfra Rift in Iceland: The Silfra Rift, a fissure between the

North American and Eurasian tectonic plates, offers unique underwater visibility and is a popular site for scuba diving, providing a literal touch between two continents.

The Exploration of the Black Sea: The Black Sea's anoxic layer (water without oxygen) has preserved ancient shipwrecks and artifacts, offering a unique glimpse into early maritime history.

The Atocha Shipwreck Discovery: The wreck of the Spanish treasure galleon Nuestra Señora de Atocha, sunk in 1622, was discovered in 1985 off the coast of Key West, Florida, yielding one of the most significant treasures ever recovered from the sea.

Oceanographic Research Vessels: Ships like the RV Knorr, which discovered the Titanic, and the RV Petrel, used in recent high-profile wreck discoveries, play a crucial role in advancing underwater exploration.

The Baltic Sea Anomaly: Discovered in 2011, the Baltic Sea Anomaly is a 60-meter-diameter circular rock-like formation on the sea floor that has sparked various theories and speculations about its origin.

Historical Artifacts & Treasures

The Rosetta Stone: Discovered in 1799, the Rosetta Stone was key to deciphering Egyptian hieroglyphs, bridging the gap between ancient and modern understanding of Egyptian culture.

The Terracotta Army: Unearthed in 1974 in Xi'an, China, the Terracotta Army consists of thousands of life-sized clay soldiers buried with the first Emperor of China, Qin Shi Huang, believed to protect him in the afterlife.

The Dead Sea Scrolls: Found in the Qumran Caves near the Dead Sea, these ancient Jewish religious manuscripts are significant for their insights into the Bible and the history of Judaism.

Tutankhamun's Tomb: Discovered in 1922 by Howard Carter, the nearly intact tomb of the young pharaoh Tutankhamun is one of the most significant archaeological discoveries, providing a wealth of information about ancient Egyptian royal burials and practices.

The Sutton Hoo Ship Burial: Uncovered in England in 1939, the Sutton Hoo ship burial dates back to the early 7th century and is one of the most important finds for understanding Anglo-Saxon England.

The Antikythera Mechanism: This ancient Greek device, discovered in a shipwreck near the island of Antikythera in 1901, is an early form of a mechanical computer used for astronomical calculations.

The Lascaux Cave Paintings: Discovered in 1940 in France, these Paleolithic cave paintings are estimated to be over 17,000 years old and offer a unique glimpse into prehistoric life.

The Mask of Agamemnon: Discovered by Heinrich Schliemann in 1876 at Mycenae in Greece, this gold funeral mask was originally believed to belong to the legendary Greek king Agamemnon but is now thought to date from an earlier period.

The Elgin Marbles: These classical Greek marble sculptures, brought to Britain in the early 19th century by Lord Elgin, were originally part of the Parthenon and other buildings on the Acropolis of Athens.

The Vinland Map: Believed by some to be a 15th-century mappa mundi, depicting part of North America long before Columbus' voyages, the Vinland Map has been a subject of controversy and debate over its authenticity.

The Moai of Easter Island: The Moai are massive stone statues on Easter Island, created by the Rapa Nui people. Their construction and transportation remain a subject of archaeological debate and fascination.

The Cyrus Cylinder: Dating back to the 6th century BC, the Cyrus Cylinder was discovered in the ruins of Babylon in modern Iraq. It is often referred to as the first declaration of human rights, highlighting the policies of Persian King Cyrus the Great after he conquered Babylon.

The Nefertiti Bust: Discovered in 1912 by German archaeologist Ludwig Borchardt, the Nefertiti Bust is a painted stucco-coated limestone bust of the Egyptian queen Nefertiti and is a notable artifact of ancient Egyptian art.

The Shroud of Turin: Believed by some to be the burial shroud of Jesus of Nazareth, the Shroud of Turin is one of the most studied and controversial artifacts in human history due to the debate over its authenticity.

The Ardagh Chalice: Found in 1868 by two boys in Ireland, the Ardagh Chalice is an example of 8th-century metalwork and one of the most important pieces of early Christian Irish Insular art.

The Voynich Manuscript: The Voynich Manuscript, a book written in an unknown script and dating back to the 15th century, is famous for being indecipherable. It has been studied by numerous cryptographers, including American and British codebreakers from both World Wars.

The Caves of Altamira: Located in Spain, the Caves of Altamira house some of the finest prehistoric art in the world, dating back to the Upper Paleolithic period. The paintings of bison and other animals are remarkably detailed and expressive.

The Sarcophagus of King Pacal: The sarcophagus in the Temple of the Inscriptions in Palenque, Mexico, is famous for its intricate carvings and the tomb of the Maya ruler K'inich Janaab' Pakal, offering insights into ancient Mayan civilization.

The Stone Spheres of Costa Rica: Discovered in the Diquis Delta of Costa Rica, these stone spheres, created by the Diquis culture, range in size and are perfectly spherical, leading to various theories about their purpose and creation.

The Liberty Bell: An iconic symbol of American independence, the Liberty Bell was originally cast in 1752 for the Pennsylvania State House. It gained iconic status when abolitionists adopted it as a symbol of the movement to end slavery.

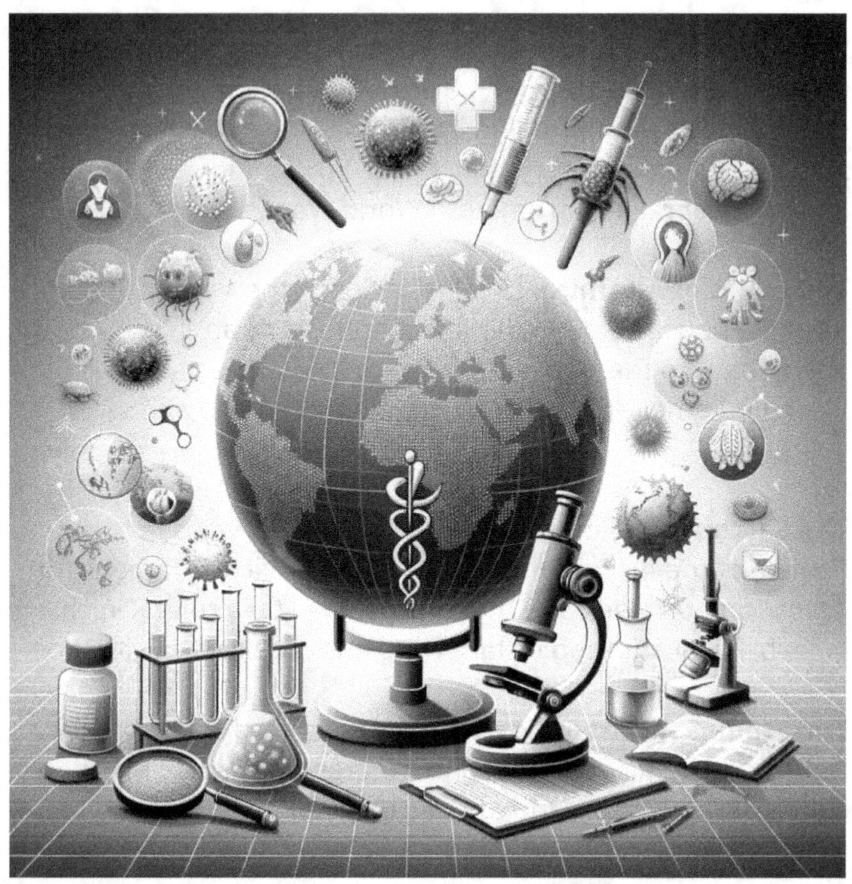

Global Health and Diseases

The Eradication of Smallpox: In 1980, smallpox was declared eradicated by the World Health Organization (WHO), marking a significant triumph for global public health. It remains the only human disease to have been eradicated.

The Discovery of Penicillin: Alexander Fleming's accidental discovery of penicillin in 1928 revolutionized medicine by introducing the age of antibiotics, dramatically reducing deaths from bacterial infections.

The HIV/AIDS Epidemic: Identified in the early 1980s, HIV/AIDS has had a profound global impact. Antiretroviral therapy, introduced in 1996, has transformed HIV from a fatal diagnosis to a manageable chronic condition for many.

The Polio Vaccine: Developed by Jonas Salk and first tested in 1952, the polio vaccine has led to the near-eradication of polio, a disease that once caused widespread paralysis and death.

The Spanish Flu Pandemic of 1918: One of the deadliest pandemics in history, the Spanish flu infected one-third of the world's population and killed an estimated 50 million people.

The Rise of Non-Communicable Diseases: In recent decades, there has been an increasing global focus on non-communicable diseases (NCDs) like heart disease, cancer, and diabetes, which are now the leading causes of death worldwide.

The Ebola Outbreaks: Ebola, a viral hemorrhagic fever, first emerged in 1976. The 2014-2016 outbreak in West Africa was the largest and most complex Ebola outbreak since the virus was discovered.

The Human Genome Project: Completed in 2003, the Human Genome Project mapped the entire human genome. This breakthrough has enormous implications for understanding and treating genetic diseases.

The SARS-CoV-2 Pandemic: Beginning in late 2019, the COVID-19 pandemic caused by the novel coronavirus SARS-

CoV-2 has led to a global health crisis, underscoring the importance of pandemic preparedness and response.

The Global Fight Against Malaria: Efforts to combat malaria, a disease transmitted by mosquito bites, have intensified in the 21st century, with significant reductions in global malaria death rates due to better prevention and treatment.

The BCG Vaccine for Tuberculosis: Developed in the 1920s, the Bacillus Calmette-Guérin (BCG) vaccine is one of the oldest vaccines still in use and the only vaccine available for tuberculosis, a disease that continues to be a major health issue globally.

The Influenza Pandemic of 1957-1958: Also known as the Asian Flu, this global pandemic was caused by an H2N2 virus and resulted in an estimated one million to two million deaths worldwide, demonstrating the ongoing threat of influenza viruses.

Dr. Jonas Salk and the Polio Vaccine: Dr. Jonas Salk's development of the inactivated polio vaccine in the 1950s marked a turning point in the fight against poliomyelitis, a crippling and potentially deadly infectious disease.

The Discovery of Insulin: In 1921, Frederick Banting and Charles Best discovered insulin, revolutionizing the treatment of diabetes. Before insulin, diabetes was often a fatal diagnosis.

The Rise of Antimicrobial Resistance: The increasing prevalence of antibiotic-resistant bacteria poses a significant threat to global health, underscoring the need for prudent use of antibiotics and the development of new treatments.

The World Health Organization (WHO): Established in 1948, the WHO plays a critical role in global health, leading international efforts to combat diseases and improve health systems worldwide.

The Zika Virus Outbreak: The Zika virus outbreak in 2015-2016, primarily in the Americas, brought attention to this mosquito-borne disease, particularly its association with birth defects when pregnant women are infected.

The Global Fund to Fight AIDS, Tuberculosis, and Malaria: Founded in 2002, this international financing organization aims to attract, leverage, and invest in resources to combat these three significant diseases.

Mental Health Awareness: There has been a growing global recognition of the importance of mental health, with efforts to destigmatize mental illness and improve mental health services around the world.

Vaccination Campaigns and the Elimination of Diseases: Global vaccination campaigns have been crucial in reducing the prevalence of, and in some cases eliminating, diseases such as measles, rubella, and neonatal tetanus in many parts of the world.

Rare Animals & Conservation

The Giant Panda's Conservation Success Story: Once near extinction, the giant panda has become a symbol of wildlife conservation, thanks in part to concerted efforts by China and organizations like the WWF. Its status improved from "Endangered" to "Vulnerable" due to effective forest protection and reforestation.

The Discovery of the Coelacanth: Thought to have been extinct for 65 million years, the coelacanth, a rare order of fish, was rediscovered in 1938 off the coast of South Africa. This discovery was a significant zoological find, providing insights into the evolutionary history of vertebrates.

The Snow Leopard's Elusive Nature: Snow leopards, native to the mountain ranges of Central and South Asia, are known for their elusive nature. They are endangered due to habitat loss, poaching, and retaliatory killings by herders.

The Kakapo's Recovery Efforts: The kakapo, a flightless parrot from New Zealand, is one of the rarest birds in the world. Conservation efforts, including predator-free island sanctuaries and breeding programs, have been crucial in preventing its extinction.

The Amur Leopard's Critical Endangerment: The Amur leopard, native to the Russian Far East and China, is one of the world's most endangered big cats, with only around 100 individuals remaining in the wild due to habitat loss and poaching.

The Vaquita and Marine Conservation: The vaquita, a small porpoise found in the northern part of the Gulf of California, is the most endangered marine mammal. Conservation efforts include habitat protection and anti-poaching measures.

The Role of Seed Banks in Plant Conservation: Seed banks, like the Svalbard Global Seed Vault in Norway, play a critical role in conserving plant diversity, especially for rare and endangered plant species.

The Black Rhino's Fight Against Extinction: Black rhinos have been brought back from the brink of extinction through conservation efforts, although they remain critically endangered due to poaching and habitat loss.

The Jane Goodall Institute and Chimpanzee Conservation: Founded by renowned primatologist Jane Goodall, the institute focuses on chimpanzee conservation and community-centered conservation programs in Africa.

The California Condor's Remarkable Comeback: The California condor, a North American bird, faced extinction in the 20th century but has made a remarkable comeback due to captive breeding programs and meticulous management in the wild.

The Blue Whale's Conservation Status: The blue whale, the largest animal known to have ever existed, saw its population severely depleted due to whaling. International protection efforts have helped its numbers increase, but it remains endangered.

The Revival of the American Bison: Once nearly extinct due to overhunting and habitat loss, conservation efforts, including national legislation and breeding programs, have helped restore bison populations in North America.

The Lord Howe Island Stick Insect's Comeback: Presumed extinct since the 1920s, the Lord Howe Island stick insect was rediscovered in 2001. Conservationists have since established successful breeding programs to revive its population.

The Orangutan's Habitat Crisis: Orangutans, native to

Indonesia and Malaysia, are critically endangered largely due to deforestation and land conversion for palm oil plantations. Conservation initiatives are focusing on habitat protection and anti-poaching measures.

The Axolotl's Unique Regeneration Abilities: Endemic to Mexico, the axolotl is not only rare but also fascinating for its ability to regenerate limbs. It faces threats from habitat loss and water pollution.

The Conservation of Coral Reefs: Coral reefs, like Australia's Great Barrier Reef, are vital ecosystems that support a diverse range of marine life. Climate change, ocean acidification, and human activities pose significant threats to these underwater habitats.

The Gharial's Narrow Habitat Range: The gharial, a crocodile native to the Indian subcontinent, is critically endangered, with fewer than 250 mature individuals remaining. Conservation efforts focus on habitat protection and reducing fishing net casualties.

Project Tiger in India: Launched in 1973, Project Tiger has been a successful wildlife conservation venture in India, significantly increasing the population of the Bengal tiger through various protective measures.

The Golden Lion Tamarin's Reintroduction Success: The golden lion tamarin, native to Brazil, has been the focus of successful reintroduction programs, which have helped to increase its numbers in the wild.

The Saola's Discovery and Conservation: Sometimes called the "Asian unicorn," the saola was discovered in Vietnam in 1992 and is critically endangered. Conservation efforts are hampered by the animal's elusiveness and the remoteness of its habitat.

Ancient Mythologies & Legends

Greek Mythology - The Pantheon of Gods: Greek mythology features a complex pantheon, including Zeus, the king of gods; Poseidon, the god of the sea; and Athena, the goddess of wisdom. These stories often explore themes of heroism, morality, and the human condition.

Norse Mythology - Ragnarök: In Norse legends, Ragnarök is a series of events leading to the death of major figures like Odin, Thor, and Loki, followed by the world's rebirth. These tales were a central part of Viking culture and belief.

Egyptian Mythology - The Afterlife: Ancient Egyptian beliefs centered significantly on the afterlife, with gods like Osiris and Anubis playing key roles in the journey of the soul after death. The Book of the Dead was a guide for the deceased to navigate the afterlife.

Hindu Mythology - The Epics: Hindu mythology includes epic tales like the Mahabharata and Ramayana, which explore themes of dharma (duty/righteousness) and karma. These texts have had a profound influence on Indian culture and spirituality.

The Legend of King Arthur: This British legend, including figures like King Arthur, Merlin the wizard, and the Knights of the Round Table, has been a significant part of Western literature, exploring themes of chivalry, betrayal, and love.

Chinese Mythology - The Dragon: In Chinese culture, the dragon is a symbol of power, strength, and good luck. Dragons are often depicted as benevolent creatures in contrast to Western mythologies.

Japanese Mythology - The Kami: Shinto, the indigenous spirituality of Japan, involves the worship of kami, spirits associated with natural elements, objects, and ancestors. These beliefs are deeply ingrained in Japanese culture.

The Aztec Mythology: The Aztecs had a rich pantheon of gods, with Huitzilopochtli, the god of sun and war, and

Quetzalcoatl, the feathered serpent god, being central. Their myths often included creation stories and rituals of sacrifice.

African Mythologies - Diverse Traditions: African myths and legends are incredibly diverse, reflecting the continent's vast array of cultures. They often include creation myths, trickster stories, and tales explaining natural phenomena.

The Epic of Gilgamesh: One of the earliest known works of literature, the Epic of Gilgamesh from ancient Mesopotamia, explores themes of friendship, the pursuit of fame, and the quest for eternal life.

Roman Mythology - The Foundation of Rome: According to legend, the city of Rome was founded by the twin brothers Romulus and Remus, who were raised by a she-wolf. Roman mythology often parallels Greek myths but with distinct names and attributes for gods and heroes.

Celtic Mythology - The Legend of the Tuatha Dé Danann: In Irish mythology, the Tuatha Dé Danann are a race of supernaturally-gifted people. They are central to many Irish mythological tales and symbolize the magic and spirituality of ancient Ireland.

The Legend of El Dorado: This South American legend, originating in the 16th century, spoke of a city or a king rich in gold and jewels, leading many explorers on futile quests through the jungles of South America.

Native American Myths - The Trickster: Many Native American cultures have stories of a trickster, a god, spirit, man, or animal who breaks the rules of the gods or nature, often with humorous or disastrous results. Trickster tales are used to teach moral lessons and cultural values.

The Sumerian Epic of Gilgamesh: One of the oldest known works of literature, this epic from ancient Mesopotamia follows the adventures of Gilgamesh, a historical king, and his quest for immortality, exploring themes of friendship, grief, and the human condition.

Australian Aboriginal Dreamtime Stories: These stories are a key part of Aboriginal culture, explaining the origins and culture of the land and its people. They encompass the creation of the world, its major landmarks, and the creation of people.

The Finnish Kalevala: Compiled in the 19th century from oral folklore and mythology, the Kalevala is a national epic of Finland. It played a significant role in the development of the Finnish national identity.

Slavic Mythology - Baba Yaga: A famous figure in Slavic folklore, Baba Yaga is depicted as a hag who flies around in a mortar, wielding a pestle. She is a complex character, sometimes helping and other times hindering those who encounter her.

The Myths of Atlantis: First mentioned by Plato, the legend of Atlantis has captivated the imagination for centuries. Described as a technologically advanced utopian society that ultimately fell out of favor with the gods, it's a symbol of civilizations lost to time.

The Legend of the Minotaur in Greek Mythology: The

Minotaur, a creature with the head of a bull and the body of a man, was said to dwell in the Labyrinth on Crete, a complex maze constructed for King Minos.

Influential Leaders in History

Alexander the Great's Conquests: Alexander the Great, the King of Macedonia, is known for creating one of the largest empires of the ancient world by the age of thirty. His conquests spread Greek culture throughout the known world, significantly influencing the subsequent Roman Empire.

Cleopatra's Reign in Egypt: Cleopatra, the last active ruler of the Ptolemaic Kingdom of Egypt, was known for her intelligence and political astuteness, as well as her relationships with Roman leaders Julius Caesar and Mark Antony.

Genghis Khan's Mongol Empire: Genghis Khan founded the Mongol Empire, which became the largest contiguous empire in history after his death. His leadership style and military strategies are still studied today.

Queen Elizabeth I and the Elizabethan Era: Queen Elizabeth I's reign is known as the Elizabethan Era, famous for the flourishing of English drama, led by playwrights such as William Shakespeare, and the exploration and colonization of the New World.

Napoleon Bonaparte's Influence on Europe: A military leader and emperor, Napoleon Bonaparte dominated European and global affairs for more than a decade while leading France against a series of coalitions in the Napoleonic Wars.

Mahatma Gandhi's Nonviolent Resistance: Mahatma Gandhi was a leader in India's struggle for independence from British rule, famous for his philosophy of nonviolent resistance, which has inspired civil rights movements worldwide.

Martin Luther King Jr.'s Leadership in the Civil Rights Movement: An American Baptist minister and activist, Martin Luther King Jr. was a leader in the American civil rights movement, advocating for nonviolent resistance and delivering his iconic "I Have a Dream" speech.

Winston Churchill's Leadership during World War II: As Prime Minister of the United Kingdom, Winston Churchill's leadership, oratory, and writings during World War II were crucial to the British war effort.

Nelson Mandela's Fight Against Apartheid: Nelson Mandela, South Africa's first black president, is renowned for his role in ending apartheid and fostering reconciliation in South Africa.

Joan of Arc's Role in the Hundred Years' War: A French peasant girl, Joan of Arc became a military leader and national heroine of France for her role during the Lancastrian phase of the Hundred Years' War against England.

Emperor Ashoka's Rule in India: Ashoka the Great, the third emperor of the Maurya Dynasty in India, is celebrated for spreading Buddhism and promoting non-violence after witnessing the bloodshed of war.

Queen Victoria's Long Reign: Queen Victoria, who reigned over the United Kingdom for 63 years, oversaw a period of industrial, cultural, political, scientific, and military change within the United Kingdom and was a symbol of the British Empire.

Julius Caesar's Impact on Rome: A pivotal figure in the transition from the Roman Republic to the Roman Empire, Julius Caesar's leadership, military achievements, and eventual dictatorship changed the course of Roman history.

Eleanor Roosevelt's Humanitarian Work: As the First Lady of the United States during President Franklin D. Roosevelt's four terms, Eleanor Roosevelt was a strong advocate for civil rights and women's rights, and she played a significant role in drafting the Universal Declaration of Human Rights.

Abraham Lincoln and the American Civil War: As the 16th President of the United States, Abraham Lincoln led the nation through its Civil War and worked to end slavery in the United States.

Catherine the Great's Reign in Russia: As the longest-ruling female leader of Russia, Catherine the Great expanded the Russian Empire, improved administration, and vigorously promoted the arts and education.

Atatürk's Modernization of Turkey: Mustafa Kemal Atatürk, the founder of the Republic of Turkey, implemented comprehensive political, economic, and cultural reforms, transforming Turkey into a modern, secular, and national state.

Emperor Constantine's Influence on Christianity: Constantine the Great, as Roman emperor, played a crucial role in the spread of Christianity by legalizing it throughout the Roman Empire and calling the First Council of Nicaea.

Charlemagne's Reign and the Carolingian Renaissance: As the King of the Franks and later Emperor of the Romans, Charlemagne united much of Western Europe and stimulated a cultural and intellectual revival known as the Carolingian Renaissance.

The Leadership of Saladin in the Crusades: A Muslim military leader, Saladin is known for his leadership during the Crusades, particularly for recapturing Jerusalem from the

Crusaders, and is respected for his chivalry and humanity in warfare.

Alexander Hamilton's Impact on American Finance: As one of the Founding Fathers of the United States, Alexander Hamilton was instrumental in establishing the national banking system and had a significant influence on the country's early financial policies.

Empress Wu Zetian's Rule in China: Wu Zetian, the only woman in Chinese history to rule as an emperor, was known for her effective and ambitious rule in the Tang dynasty, significantly expanding the Chinese empire.

Simon Bolivar's Role in Latin American Independence: Known as El Libertador, Simon Bolivar was a military and political leader who played a key role in liberating much of South America from Spanish rule.

Theodore Roosevelt's Progressive Policies: As the 26th President of the United States, Theodore Roosevelt was known for his progressive policies, including environmental conservation efforts, and his role in negotiating the end of the Russo-Japanese War.

Catherine de' Medici's Influence in France: As queen consort and regent of France, Catherine de' Medici played a key role in the political machinations of the French Wars of Religion, influencing the course of French history.

Otto von Bismarck's Unification of Germany: Often referred to as the "Iron Chancellor," Otto von Bismarck was the driving force behind the unification of Germany and the establishment of the German Empire in the late 19th century.

Emperor Meiji's Modernization of Japan: Under Emperor Meiji, Japan underwent a rapid transformation from a feudal society to a modern industrial state, embracing Western ideas and technology.

Suleiman the Magnificent's Ottoman Empire: Suleiman the Magnificent expanded the Ottoman Empire to its zenith, known for his military prowess, legal reforms, and fostering of arts and culture.

Elizabeth Cady Stanton's Advocacy for Women's Rights: A leading figure in the early women's rights movement in the United States, Elizabeth Cady Stanton was instrumental in initiating the first women's rights and suffrage movements in the U.S.

Frederick Douglass' Abolitionist Work: An escaped slave, Frederick Douglass became a national leader of the abolitionist movement in the United States, known for his oratory and antislavery writings.

Revolutionary Technologies

The Invention of the Wheel: The wheel, invented in ancient Mesopotamia around 3500 B.C., revolutionized transportation and led to significant advancements in agriculture and trade.

The Steam Engine and the Industrial Revolution: The development of the steam engine in the 18th century by inventors like James Watt fueled the Industrial Revolution, changing manufacturing, transportation, and global economics.

Electricity's Transformative Impact: The harnessing of electricity in the 19th century, with key figures like Thomas Edison and Nikola Tesla, revolutionized the way people live and work, leading to the modern age of technology.

The Telephone's Communication Revolution: Invented by Alexander Graham Bell in 1876, the telephone transformed personal and business communication, shrinking distances and connecting the world in unprecedented ways.

The Advent of Personal Computing: The personal computer, popularized in the 1970s and 1980s by companies like Apple and IBM, changed the way people process information, communicate, and entertain themselves.

The Birth of the Internet: Originally developed as a project for the U.S. Department of Defense, the internet has become the backbone of global communication, information exchange, and commerce.

The Smartphone Revolution: The launch of smartphones, particularly the iPhone in 2007, created a new era of mobile computing, drastically changing communication, media consumption, and daily life.

The Development of Artificial Intelligence: Advances in AI and machine learning are transforming industries, from healthcare and transportation to entertainment and customer service.

The Discovery of Penicillin and Modern Medicine: The

accidental discovery of penicillin by Alexander Fleming in 1928 ushered in the era of antibiotics, revolutionizing the treatment of bacterial infections.

Space Exploration Technologies: The development of rocket technology and space exploration, highlighted by the Apollo moon landings and the International Space Station, has expanded human understanding of the universe.

The Invention of the Printing Press: Johannes Gutenberg's invention of the printing press in the 15th century democratized knowledge, making books and information accessible to a much wider audience and sparking significant cultural and religious transformations.

The Development of Vaccination: Edward Jenner's development of the smallpox vaccine in 1796 marked the beginning of the practice of vaccination, a medical breakthrough that has saved countless lives by preventing infectious diseases.

The Creation of the World Wide Web: Invented by Tim Berners-Lee in 1989, the World Wide Web transformed the internet from a niche technology into a global phenomenon, fundamentally changing how information is shared and consumed.

The Airplane and Modern Aviation: The Wright brothers' first powered flight in 1903 laid the groundwork for modern aviation, shrinking the world by enabling faster and more efficient travel across long distances.

Blockchain Technology: Initially developed to support Bitcoin, a digital cryptocurrency, blockchain technology has emerged as a revolutionary way of maintaining secure and decentralized records, with potential applications in various industries.

The Discovery of DNA's Structure: James Watson and Francis Crick's identification of the double helix structure of DNA in 1953 revolutionized the field of genetics, paving the way for advances in biotechnology and medicine.

The Advent of 3D Printing: 3D printing technology, which allows for the creation of three-dimensional objects from digital designs, is transforming manufacturing, healthcare, and even space exploration.

The Green Revolution in Agriculture: The Green Revolution, which began in the 1940s, introduced high-yielding crop varieties and advanced agricultural techniques, significantly increasing global food production and averting widespread famine.

Renewable Energy Technologies: The development of renewable energy technologies like solar panels, wind turbines, and hydroelectric power is playing a crucial role in addressing global energy needs and combating climate change.

The Introduction of the Integrated Circuit: The invention of the integrated circuit, or microchip, by Jack Kilby and Robert Noyce in the 1950s, is fundamental to modern electronics, enabling the miniaturization and efficiency of electronic devices.

The Human Brain & Neuroscience

The Brain's Astonishing Complexity: Comprising about 86 billion neurons, each with thousands of synaptic connections, the human brain is an extraordinarily complex organ. This complexity enables the vast range of human thoughts, emotions, and behaviors.

Neuroplasticity's Revolutionary Discovery: Neuroplasticity, the brain's ability to reorganize itself by forming new neural connections, revolutionized our understanding of the brain. It shows that our brains are not static and can adapt to new learning and experiences throughout life.

Phineas Gage's Incredible Survival: In 1848, Phineas Gage survived a severe brain injury when an iron rod penetrated his skull. His survival and subsequent personality changes provided early evidence of the brain's role in personality and behavior.

The Mystery of Consciousness: Consciousness, the state of being aware of and able to think and perceive, remains one of the greatest mysteries in neuroscience. Its study combines elements of psychology, philosophy, and neurology, reflecting the brain's complex nature.

The Brain's Role in Emotions: The limbic system, a set of brain structures including the amygdala and hippocampus, plays a crucial role in our emotional responses. Understanding these structures sheds light on emotional disorders and treatments.

Mirror Neurons and Empathy: Discovered in the 1990s, mirror neurons fire both when an individual acts and when they observe the same action performed by another. This mirroring process is thought to be crucial for understanding others' actions and intentions, and for developing empathy.

The Impact of Sleep on the Brain: Sleep plays a critical role in brain function. During sleep, the brain clears out waste products and consolidates memories, highlighting the importance of sleep for overall cognitive health.

Brain-Computer Interfaces: Advancements in neuroscience have led to the development of brain-computer interfaces (BCIs), which enable direct communication between the brain and external devices. BCIs hold the potential to revolutionize treatments for neurological disorders and injuries.

The Enigma of Dreaming: Dreams, a universal human experience, are a significant area of study in neuroscience. They are thought to play roles in memory consolidation, emotional regulation, and problem-solving.

The Significance of the Prefrontal Cortex: The prefrontal cortex, responsible for complex cognitive behavior, personality expression, decision making, and moderating social behavior, is a key area in understanding human behavior and cognitive processes.

Discovery of Neurotransmitters: The identification of neurotransmitters, chemicals that transmit signals across a synapse from one neuron to another, was pivotal in understanding how the brain processes information and controls the body.

The Brain's Visual Processing Power: The human brain can process entire images seen for as little as 13 milliseconds, showcasing the incredible speed and efficiency of our visual processing capabilities.

Neurogenesis in Adults: Once believed impossible, it's now known that neurogenesis, the formation of new neurons, occurs in certain parts of the adult brain, such as the hippocampus, altering our understanding of brain aging and learning.

The Role of the Amygdala in Fear: The amygdala, a small, almond-shaped structure in the brain, plays a crucial role in processing emotions, especially fear. Studies of the amygdala have greatly informed our understanding of anxiety and phobias.

The Influence of Genetics on Brain Development: Genetics play a significant role in brain development and functioning, influencing aspects like intelligence, mental health, and the likelihood of developing neurological disorders.

The Puzzle of Left-Brain vs Right-Brain: The popular notion of people being 'left-brained' or 'right-brained' is oversimplified. While certain functions are more dominant in one hemisphere, the brain's hemispheres work together intricately.

Santiago Ramón y Cajal and Neuron Doctrine: Santiago Ramón y Cajal, a Spanish neuroscientist, made significant contributions to neuroscience, including the development of the neuron doctrine, which established that neurons are discrete cells that communicate with each other.

The Impact of Stress on the Brain: Chronic stress can have a significant impact on the brain, affecting memory and learning and increasing the risk of various mental health disorders.

Functional MRI (fMRI) and Brain Mapping: The development of functional MRI technology has allowed unprecedented insight into the active brain, enabling scientists to study brain function and map regions responsible for critical cognitive and motor functions.

World Economies and Currencies

The U.S. Dollar as a Global Reserve Currency: The United States dollar is the most widely used currency for global transactions and is the world's primary reserve currency, held by numerous governments and institutions as part of their foreign exchange reserves.

China's Rapid Economic Growth: Since initiating market

reforms in 1978, China has been among the world's fastest-growing economies, significantly increasing its global economic influence and lifting hundreds of millions of people out of poverty.

The Eurozone and the Euro: Introduced in 1999, the euro is the official currency of 19 of the 27 European Union member states, known together as the Eurozone. It's the second-largest and second-most traded currency in the foreign exchange market after the U.S. dollar.

Bitcoin and Cryptocurrencies: Bitcoin, introduced in 2009, was the first decentralized cryptocurrency. Since then, thousands of alternative cryptocurrencies with various functions and specifications have been developed.

The Great Depression and Global Impact: The Great Depression, beginning in 1929, was the deepest and longest-lasting economic downturn in the industrialized world, profoundly affecting both national economies and international trade.

OPEC's Influence on Oil Prices: The Organization of Petroleum Exporting Countries (OPEC), founded in 1960, coordinates and unifies petroleum policies among member countries and plays a significant role in determining global oil prices.

Switzerland's Banking Secrecy: Swiss banks are renowned for their banking secrecy and stability. The Swiss Banking Law of 1934 made it illegal to disclose account holder information, making Switzerland a haven for foreign capital.

The Marshall Plan's Role in European Recovery: After World War II, the Marshall Plan was an American initiative to aid Western Europe in which the U.S. gave over $12 billion in economic assistance to help rebuild Western European economies.

India's IT Services Industry: India's IT services industry is one of the fastest-growing in the world, contributing significantly to the country's GDP and exports, and marking a shift from traditional agricultural and manufacturing dominance.

The Asian Financial Crisis of 1997: The Asian Financial Crisis, which began in 1997, was a period of financial crisis that gripped much of Asia, causing currencies to plummet, devaluing stock markets and other asset prices, and precipitating a severe economic downturn.

Japan's Post-WWII Economic Miracle: After World War II, Japan experienced rapid economic growth, becoming the world's second-largest economy by the 1960s. This growth was driven by efficient manufacturing techniques, technological innovation, and government-industry cooperation.

The Gold Standard and Its Abandonment: The gold standard, once the basis for valuing many currencies, was largely abandoned in the 20th century. It linked currencies to specific amounts of gold, but was phased out to allow more flexibility in monetary policy.

African Mobile Money Revolution: In Africa, mobile money services like M-Pesa have revolutionized banking, allowing millions of people without access to traditional banks to perform transactions using their mobile phones.

The Rise of Sovereign Wealth Funds: Sovereign wealth funds, state-owned investment funds, have grown in significance, managing trillions of dollars in assets. They are major players in global financial markets, often derived from countries' natural resource revenues.

Silicon Valley's Impact on the Global Economy: Silicon Valley in California is a global center for high technology and innovation. Companies originating from this area, such as Apple, Google, and Facebook, have significantly influenced the global economy and daily life.

The Bretton Woods Agreement: Established in 1944, the Bretton Woods Agreement set up international financial institutions like the World Bank and the International Monetary Fund (IMF) and established the U.S. dollar's dominance in international trade.

The European Debt Crisis: Starting in 2009, the European debt crisis was a multi-year debt crisis in the Eurozone, where several members were unable to repay or refinance their government debt without the assistance of third parties.

Singapore's Economic Transformation: Singapore's transformation from a developing to a developed country in a single generation is a significant economic success story. Its strategic location, efficient government, and business-friendly environment have been key to its growth.

The 2008 Global Financial Crisis: Triggered by the collapse of the housing bubble in the United States, the 2008 financial crisis had a severe worldwide economic impact. It led to the Great Recession, with lasting effects on global markets and economies.

The Rise of the Gig Economy: The gig economy, characterized by flexible, temporary, or freelance jobs, often involving connecting with clients or customers through an online platform, has grown rapidly, changing traditional employment models.

Famous Bridges & Structures

Golden Gate Bridge's Art Deco Design: San Francisco's Golden Gate Bridge, completed in 1937, is an iconic Art Deco marvel. Its distinctive "International Orange" color was chosen for visibility in San Francisco's foggy weather.

Tower Bridge's Victorian Gothic Style: London's Tower Bridge, a symbol of the city, combines a bascule and suspension bridge. It's recognized for its Victorian Gothic style, a contrast to the nearby Tower of London.

Sydney Harbour Bridge's Record-Breaking Span: Known as "The Coathanger," Sydney Harbour Bridge is the world's largest steel arch bridge. Its construction in 1932 was a significant engineering feat, involving over 52,800 tons of steel.

The Eiffel Tower as a Cultural Icon: The Eiffel Tower, constructed for the 1889 World's Fair in Paris, was initially criticized for its design but has become a global cultural icon and one of the most recognizable structures in the world.

The Colosseum's Ancient Engineering: Rome's Colosseum, completed in 80 AD, could hold up to 80,000 spectators. This ancient amphitheater's design and complex system of vaults were groundbreaking in the history of architecture.

Burj Khalifa's Record Height: Standing at 828 meters, Dubai's Burj Khalifa is the tallest structure and building in the world since its completion in 2010. It's a symbol of Dubai's rapid development and architectural ambition.

Brooklyn Bridge's Engineering Breakthrough: New York City's Brooklyn Bridge was the world's first steel-wire suspension bridge when completed in 1883. Its construction was a milestone in architectural history, linking Manhattan and Brooklyn.

Great Wall of China's Immense Scale: Stretching over 13,000 miles, the Great Wall of China is the world's longest wall and biggest ancient architecture. Its construction spanned over several dynasties, beginning as early as the 7th century BC.

Machu Picchu's Incan Mystery: Peru's Machu Picchu, an Incan citadel set high in the Andes Mountains, was built in the 15th century. Its precise stone construction without the use of mortar remains an archaeological wonder.

Petra's Rock-Cut Architecture: Petra, an archaeological site in Jordan, is famous for its rock-cut architecture and water conduit system. This ancient city, carved into pink sandstone cliffs, dates back to as early as 300 BC.

The Leaning Tower of Pisa's Accidental Tilt: Italy's Leaning Tower of Pisa is famous for its unintended tilt. Construction began in 1173, and the tower began to lean during construction due to a weak foundation, becoming a unique symbol of architectural eccentricity.

The Hoover Dam's Massive Concrete Volume: The Hoover Dam, located on the border between Arizona and Nevada, is one of the world's largest concrete structures and hydroelectric power plants, completed in 1936. It holds back America's largest reservoir, Lake Mead.

Sagrada Família's Ongoing Construction: Barcelona's Sagrada Família, a basilica designed by Antoni Gaudí, has been under construction since 1882. Known for its elaborate Gothic and Art Nouveau forms, it's a testament to enduring architectural ambition.

The Panama Canal's Engineering Feat: The Panama Canal, completed in 1914, is a 50-mile waterway that connects the Atlantic and Pacific Oceans. Its construction was one of the most challenging engineering projects ever undertaken.

The Shard's Vertical City Concept: London's The Shard, completed in 2012, is the tallest building in the UK. Its design represents a vertical city and includes offices, restaurants, and a viewing gallery.

Christ the Redeemer's Iconic Statue: Overlooking Rio de Janeiro, the Christ the Redeemer statue, completed in 1931, stands 30 meters tall. It is one of the New Seven Wonders of the World and a symbol of Brazilian Christianity.

The Trans-Siberian Railway's Vast Network: Stretching over 9,289 kilometers, the Trans-Siberian Railway is the longest railway line in the world. It connects Moscow with the Russian Far East and the Sea of Japan.

The CN Tower's Sky-High Observation Deck: Once the world's tallest freestanding structure, Toronto's CN Tower features the world's highest glass floor paneled elevator and a sky-high observation deck offering expansive views of the city.

The Channel Tunnel's Undersea Passage: The Channel Tunnel, completed in 1994, is a 50.45-kilometer railway tunnel beneath the English Channel, linking the UK and France. It's one of the longest underwater tunnels in the world.

The Space Needle's Futuristic Design: Seattle's Space Needle, built for the 1962 World's Fair, features a futuristic design and stands 184 meters tall. It symbolizes innovation and was built to withstand strong winds and earthquakes.

Rock and Roll

Elvis Presley - The King of Rock and Roll: Elvis Presley, often referred to as "The King of Rock and Roll," revolutionized music in the 1950s with his energetic performances and unique sound, blending rhythm and blues with country.

The Beatles' Global Impact: The Beatles, hailing from Liverpool, England, not only led the British Invasion of the US music market but also became one of the best-selling music acts in history, transforming the landscape of rock music.

Jimi Hendrix's Guitar Mastery: Jimi Hendrix, known for his innovative electric guitar playing, redefined the role of the guitar in rock music. His performance of the "Star-Spangled Banner" at Woodstock in 1969 remains one of the most iconic moments in rock history.

The Rolling Stones' Longevity: Formed in 1962, The Rolling Stones are renowned for their fusion of blues and rock music. Their longevity and continued success have made them one of the longest-performing rock bands in history.

Led Zeppelin's Heavy Metal Foundations: Led Zeppelin's powerful and innovative music in the late 1960s and 1970s laid the foundation for the development of heavy metal, marking a new era in rock music.

Woodstock Music Festival of 1969: The Woodstock Music Festival, held in August 1969, became a symbol of the counterculture movement. It attracted an audience of over 400,000 people and featured legendary performances by artists like Janis Joplin and The Who.

Punk Rock's Rebellion: Emerging in the 1970s, punk rock, with bands like The Ramones and The Sex Pistols, was a reaction against mainstream rock, characterized by its fast-paced music and rebellious attitude.

MTV's Influence on Rock Music: Launched in 1981, MTV revolutionized the music industry by placing a new emphasis on the visual presentation of music, greatly impacting the rock genre with iconic music videos.

Grunge Movement of the Early 90s: The grunge movement, led by bands like Nirvana and Pearl Jam, emerged from Seattle in the early 1990s. It was marked by its raw sound and disenchanted lyrics, reshaping the rock music scene.

Queen and Live Aid Performance: Queen's performance at Live Aid in 1985, particularly their rendition of "Bohemian Rhapsody," is often considered one of the greatest live performances in the history of rock music.

Rock and Roll Hall of Fame: Established in 1983 and located in Cleveland, Ohio, the Rock and Roll Hall of Fame honors the most influential artists, producers, and other figures who have had a major influence on the development of rock and roll.

Fleetwood Mac's Unique Sound: Fleetwood Mac, formed in 1967, is known for their unique blend of British blues, pop, and soft rock, with their album "Rumours" being one of the best-selling albums of all time.

The Influence of The Beach Boys: The Beach Boys, emerging in the 1960s, are celebrated for their harmonious sound and innovative compositions, particularly the album "Pet Sounds," which greatly influenced the evolution of rock music.

Bob Dylan's Songwriting Genius: Bob Dylan, an influential figure in popular music and culture for more than five decades, is renowned for his profound songwriting, which blended rock music with folk, blues, and poetic lyrics.

Pink Floyd's Concept Albums: Known for their philosophical lyrics, sonic experimentation, and elaborate live shows, Pink

Floyd's concept albums, like "The Dark Side of the Moon," have left a lasting impact on the rock genre.

Bruce Springsteen's Americana Rock: Bruce Springsteen, nicknamed "The Boss," is known for his poetic lyrics, distinctive voice, and energetic stage performances. His music often explores the lives, struggles, and dreams of American working-class people.

U2's Global Activism and Sound: Irish rock band U2, formed in 1976, is known not only for their unique sound and Bono's distinctive vocals but also for their activism, focusing on human rights and social justice issues.

Metallica's Thrash Metal Influence: Metallica, formed in 1981, played a significant role in popularizing thrash metal. Their albums like "Master of Puppets" are considered landmarks in the genre of heavy metal.

AC/DC's Hard Rock Legacy: Australian band AC/DC, known for their raw and powerful hard rock, have sustained a successful career since the 1970s. Their album "Back in Black" is one of the best-selling albums by any band.

The Rise of Alternative Rock in the 90s: Bands like Radiohead and Red Hot Chili Peppers led the alternative rock movement in the 1990s, offering diverse sounds that deviated from mainstream rock music.

Green Day and Punk Revival: Green Day, formed in 1986, played a key role in the 1990s punk revival with their album "Dookie," bringing punk rock back to widespread popularity.

Pop Music

The Beatles' Revolutionary Impact: The Beatles not only led the British Invasion of the American music market in the 1960s but also revolutionized pop music with their innovative songwriting and recording techniques.

Michael Jackson - The King of Pop: Michael Jackson, known as the King of Pop, transformed the landscape of pop music with his groundbreaking music and iconic dance moves, particularly with his album "Thriller," the best-selling album of all time.

Madonna's Influence on Pop and Fashion: Madonna, known for her continuous reinvention and versatility in music production, songwriting, and visual presentation, has been a pop icon since the 1980s, influencing many artists and fashion trends.

The Rise of MTV and Music Videos: MTV, launched in 1981, revolutionized pop music by placing a new emphasis on the visual aspect of music, making music videos an essential component of an artist's creative expression.

Beyoncé's Commanding Presence: Beyoncé, initially rising to fame as the lead singer of Destiny's Child and later as a solo artist, is known for her powerful vocals, dynamic performances, and influential role in modern pop and R&B music.

Britney Spears' Teen Pop Phenomenon: Britney Spears became a prominent figure in the revival of teen pop in the late 1990s and early 2000s. Her debut single "...Baby One More Time" is one of the best-selling singles of all time.

Taylor Swift's Evolution as an Artist: Taylor Swift, initially known for her work in country music, successfully crossed over to pop music. Her narrative songwriting, which often centers around her personal life, has received widespread critical praise, media coverage and record breaking concert and streaming sales

K-Pop's Global Explosion: Korean Pop, or K-Pop, has become a global phenomenon, with groups like BTS and BLACKPINK achieving international fame, showcasing intricate choreography, synchronized performances, and engaging digital content.

The Evolution of Boy Bands: From The Jackson 5 in the 1970s to New Kids on the Block, Backstreet Boys, NSYNC in the 1990s, and One Direction in the 2010s, boy bands have been a recurring and popular trend in pop music.

Electronic Dance Music's Influence: Electronic Dance Music (EDM) has had a significant influence on pop music, with artists and producers incorporating its elements into their work, leading to a fusion of genres and the rise of festival culture.

Adele's Powerhouse Vocals and Emotional Depth: Adele, known for her soulful voice and emotive lyrics, has won numerous awards for her albums like "21" and "25." Her powerful ballads have resonated with a global audience, redefining the contemporary ballad.

The Global Phenomenon of Latin Pop: Artists like Shakira, Ricky Martin, and Enrique Iglesias have popularized Latin pop worldwide. This genre blends traditional Latin music with mainstream pop and has significantly influenced global pop music culture.

Lady Gaga's Artistic Versatility: Lady Gaga, known for her unconventional and provocative work as well as her visual experimentation, has been a key figure in modern pop music. Her albums and performances showcase a unique blend of pop, electronic, and dance music.

The Impact of Streaming Services: The rise of streaming services like Spotify and Apple Music has transformed how pop music is consumed and distributed, allowing artists to reach global audiences more easily than ever.

Reggae's Influence on Pop: Reggae, originating in Jamaica, has influenced many pop artists. Bob Marley, the genre's most iconic figure, brought reggae to a worldwide audience, and its rhythms and themes have been incorporated into numerous pop songs.

The Synthpop Revolution of the 80s: Bands like Depeche Mode, New Order, and The Human League were at the forefront of the synthpop movement in the 1980s, using synthesizers to create a new, electronic sound in pop music.

The Emergence of Teen Idols: Artists like Elvis Presley, The Beatles, and more recently, Justin Bieber, have been pivotal in the phenomenon of teen idols in pop music, garnering massive, dedicated fan bases.

Disco's Era and Its Influence: The disco era of the late 1970s, with artists like Donna Summer and the Bee Gees, brought a dance-centric sound to pop music and influenced the development of electronic and dance music genres.

Whitney Houston's Vocal Prowess: Whitney Houston, known for her incredible vocal range and emotive power, has been one of pop music's most revered artists. Her rendition of "I Will Always Love You" stands as one of the best-selling singles of all time.

The Boy Band and Girl Group Resurgence: The late 1990s and early 2000s saw a resurgence of boy bands and girl groups, with acts like Spice Girls, Destiny's Child, and NSYNC dominating the pop charts and influencing a new generation of artists.

Conclusion

As we conclude this journey through the pages of our fact book, we are reminded of the extraordinary tapestry of knowledge and discovery that spans across time, cultures, and disciplines. From the awe-inspiring wonders of the natural world to the ingenious creations of human invention, each chapter has offered a glimpse into the vast and intricate mosaic of our shared history and environment.

In exploring the realms of ancient civilizations, the depths of oceans, the frontiers of space, and the mysteries of the human mind, we have encountered stories of perseverance, ingenuity, and curiosity. These narratives not only illuminate the past but also shed light on our present and future, encouraging us to continue exploring, questioning, and learning.

As we close this book, let us carry forward the spirit of discovery that has propelled humanity's greatest achievements. May the facts and stories contained within these pages inspire a sense of wonder and a desire to contribute to the ever-expanding body of knowledge that defines our existence. Let us remember that every discovery and invention, every cultural artifact and natural marvel, is a stepping stone on the path of human progress, a path that we all walk together.

This fact book, a compendium of human endeavor and natural wonder, serves as a testament to our endless quest for understanding. It is a reminder that learning is a lifelong journey, one that is as vast and varied as the universe we inhabit. As we turn the final page, let us look forward to the unwritten chapters yet to come, filled with new discoveries, innovations, and stories waiting to be told. The journey of learning never truly ends, and each day brings new opportunities to expand our horizons and deepen our understanding of the world around us.

About the Author

Texas Harmon is a hobby researcher, writer, and developer with an interest in how technology shapes our world and the use of technology to enhance communication and creativity